Silk Screen Techniques

BY

J. I. Biegeleisen

Chairman, Silk Screen Department

School of Industrial Art

Author, Silk Screen Printing Process

AND

Max Arthur Cohn

DOVER PUBLICATIONS,
NEW YORK

Published in Canada by General Publishing Company, Ltd., 30 Lesmill Road, Don Mills, Toronto, Ontario.

Published in the United Kingdom by Constable and Company, Ltd., 10 Orange Street, London WC 2.

This Dover edition, first published in 1958, is a corrected and enlarged version of the work originally published by the McGraw-Hill Book Company, Inc., under the title *Silk Screen Stencilling as a Fine Art.*

Standard Book Number: 486-20433-2
Library of Congress Catalog Card Number: 58-3044

Manufactured in the United States of America
Dover Publications, Inc.
180 Varick Street
New York, N.Y. 10014

CONTENTS

CONTENTS

iv

PREFACE TO
DOVER EDITION

ſILK SCREEN TECHNIQUES is a more popular-priced edition of *Silk Screen Stencilling As a Fine Art* by the same authors, previously published by the McGraw-Hill Book Company. In its present format and under its new title the book has been reduced in price to reach a wider market.

SILK SCREEN TECHNIQUES retains all the features of the earlier version. Some of the text has been slightly revised. The body of instructional information is exactly the same, save for several added features such as an *Index* and a helpful directory of dealers of materials. Many new illustrations have been added which reflect the latest and best of contemporary serigraph print making. For these both the publishers and authors are sincerely grateful to the National Serigraph Society and to its director, Doris Meltzer. Thanks are also extended to the McGraw-Hill Book Company for relinquishing to me the copyright previously held by them.

Mr. Cirker, president of Dover Publications felt it wise to change the original title to Silk Screen Techniques. In this I concurred because the present title encompasses the entire range of stencil techniques as a fine art and as a commercial printing process.

J. I. BIEGELEISEN

April, 1958

Keys by Ray Euffa   National Serigraph Society

Origin
and Development

Robert Leland Kiley

ORIGIN
AND DEVELOPMENT

THE desire to possess a thing of beauty is as universal as some of the more prosaic instincts of mankind. The primitive artist embellished his dart thrower with carvings of antelopes and decorated the rugged walls of his bleak cave dwelling with scenes of the hunt. That yearning to surround oneself with the beautiful is an aesthetic escape from the grim realities of everyday life. Something that is hand shaped or hand printed and has the individuality of the artisan imbedded within it evokes in all of us a different reaction from the commercial products of the factory assembly line. Yet the cost of original paintings and fine prints has been too high in the past to reach the wide potential market.

Permanent and traveling art exhibitions held at museums, galleries, and community centers have in no way diminished the public's desire to own exhibition pieces. On the contrary, the delight of viewing a painting or a print that one particularly likes but cannot afford to purchase merely whets one's appetite for it. There has long been a need for a simple art process to produce color prints inexpensively for print lovers in every walk of life. Silk screen answers that need.

The silk screen process permits the production of multicolor prints heretofore prohibitive in cost. Compared with other graphic art mediums, silk screen is easily the most versatile means of quantity printing within reach of contemporary artists. With simple, inexpensive equipment, almost as portable as a drawing board, the artist has at his command the means for reproducing prints of any size on any surface in any number of colors. The quantities need be governed only by the demand for the prints, as most stencils are good for thousands of impressions. A good print can be favorably compared with the hand-painted original. Colors can be matched closely in tone and quality. No matter how many colors there are in the print, they can all be printed in good register. The silk-screen process can simulate the subtle transparent washes of a water color, the heavy impasto of an oil painting, or the qualities of a *gouache,* pastel, or wood block.

This art *nouveau* was christened the *silk screen* process, but the artists of America did not attend the christening, which took place some fifty years ago. At birth, this graphic process became the prodigal son of sign painters, display men, and show-card writers, who hailed this new arrival as a "find" and money-maker. Here was a way, they learned, of duplicating lettering and designs in any quantity in black and white or in full color. One man told another in strictest confidence of

6

this process that permits printing directly on any flat material whatever, that produces thousands of prints from one stencil, that requires no machinery, and that can make prints of any size. Traveling teachers made the rounds of sign shops and display houses and sold the "secret" to eager buyers for what they could get. In a way, whatever price was paid by sign writers for this much-sought-after information was money well spent. Display artists found that with this unique stencil process they could do production work, competing on short runs with printers and lithographers. Thus the prodigal son Silk Screen grew stronger and had more godfathers every day.

Though Silk Screen has had many godfathers, it is difficult to trace the discovery to one man. There is no record of one man's work in this field to stand beside the achievements of a Gutenberg or a Senefelder.

Silk screen as we know it today is a perfection of the early type of stencil printing used by the ancients. The discovery of stencil printing, we may say, was almost inevitable; holes caused by insects' boring through leaves may have suggested the stencil method to primitive man. A study of the early history of the Fiji Islands brings to light one of the first uses made of the stencil in printing textiles. The islanders made stencils by cutting perforations in banana leaves and then applying vegetable dyes through these openings onto bark cloth.

As civilization progressed, those interested in spreading religious dogmas employed the stencil for quantity printing of

Fig. *a.—Decorator's paper stencil*. Showing ties or bridges worked into the design to keep the integral parts of the stencil together.

Fig. *b.—Japanese stencil*. Tieless Japanese stencil showing the intricate handcut design held together by fine strands of hair.

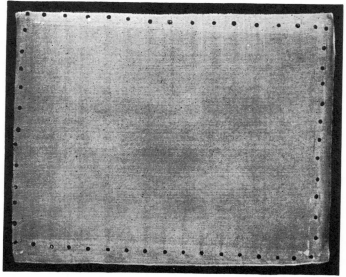

Fig. *c.—Modern silk screen*. The fine silk fabric serves as a ground to which the stencil is affixed. This eliminates the need for ties or bridges.

PLATE 1

all sorts of religious pictures and psalms. The teachings of Buddha were thus spread with stenciled *image prints*. When the Japanese adapted stenciling to their own uses for robes and decorative backgrounds, they improved it a good deal. It is difficult to comprehend how the Japanese, even with their skill and patience, could cut stencils so uncannily and with such fine detail. Their stencils were cut from specially treated paper and waterproofed to make them impervious to dyes. The Japanese craftsman cut his stencils in duplicate sheets of thin paper. The centers or loose parts of the stencil were held in permanent suspension by *ties* of superfine strands of raw silk or human hair glued to the centers and to the stencil paper. See Plate 1, Fig. *b*. Although the Japanese stencils required such painstaking care, the Oriental artists did not limit their work to single-color prints. As many as four- or five-color stencils were used in combination to print well-registered designs with fidelity of composition and color.

Stencil craft thrived even during the dark period of the Middle Ages. Strangely enough, the stencil at that time became the device of saint and sinner. Decorative stencils used in combination with wood-block printing were used to enhance such diverse subjects as image prints and playing cards. The closer communication and understanding between the East and West, as a result of conquests and crusades, spread the art of stenciling through Europe, from Germany to Spain, Italy, and France.

By the sixteenth century, stencil craft had become an established art and was used frequently in conjunction with woodblock and brush painting for religious pictures and illuminated manuscripts. These art pieces were sold at shrines to the thousands who gathered there at pilgrimages.

In England in the seventeenth century, when flocked wallpaper was at the height of fashion, the stencil was used to apply the adhesive to the paper. Fine wool flock dust was sprinkled over the sticky print to simulate appliqué or embroidery designs. In France at the beginning of the eighteenth century, Jean Papillon, the father of wallpaper, had established a thriving enterprise for the designing and printing of wallpaper by the stencil method. In America, early stencil art was practiced mostly on wallpaper and furniture. By 1787, stencils were introduced as a means of applying designs or border decorations directly onto walls. What must have been the delight of the New England artisan to find his newly whitewashed walls the welcoming canvas of stencil craft! With stencils made from oil paper, he deftly projected pictures of the Federal eagle, urns of flowers, baskets of fruit, vines, etc. onto the walls of his home. He also used the stencil extensively to decorate chairs, pianos, textiles, and many other domestic objects.

The idea of using a silk fabric as a screen or ground to hold a *tieless* stencil is generally credited to Samuel Simon of Manchester, who was granted a silk screen process patent in England in 1907.

At the outbreak of the First World War, when the production of printing was stepped up, a multicolor method was developed by John Pilsworth of San Francisco. This method, known as the *Selectasine* method, consisted of using one screen to print multicolor work by blocking out that area of the screen corresponding to the colors already printed. Commercial sign shops and display studios saw in this process the answer to the growing demand for quantity signs and posters in color. They could easily afford the equipment, and soon hundreds of shops and studios sprang up like mushrooms in soggy soil.

Craftsmen began to experiment further and developed improved means of stencilmaking. Experimentation is going on today. The use of lithographic tusche, the film method, and the photographic method of stencilmaking has expanded the scope of possibilities and narrowed the limitations of silk screen. The old type of tie stencil becomes an artistic heirloom of antiquity when compared with the modern silk screen stencil.

Silk screen is one of the important graphic arts today and has grown into an industry employing thousands of people all over the world. Besides developing into an industry in itself, one devoted to advertising, the process is also employed by so many other industries for such a variety of purposes that it is difficult to obtain actual statistics. It seems unlimited in its resources.

Silk screen is used not only to print displays, posters, show-cards, and general advertising; it is used in a thousand and one other ways. Manufacturers of furniture employ the process for decorating beds, tables, nursery furniture, etc. The textile industry has found silk screen indispensable. Large plants have been set up solely for the silk screen printing of miles of cloth. Lampshades are decorated by silk screen, and so are tea trays, rugs, book jackets, tablecloths, toys, towels, glasses, and napkins. Neckties, handbags, scarves, and practically everything that can be enhanced by design can be stenciled by the silk screen process. The phenomenal versatility of this stencil process commercialized the craft to such an extent that it was considered solely as a commercial printing process.

As the youngster Silk Screen grew older, he grew bolder and rougher. He did not always travel in the best of company; his adherents all saw in him only a means of making money. His commercial importance was emphasized while the artistic side of his nature was completely neglected. This was true until one day not so long ago, in 1938, when, after Silk Screen in the role of a fine-art process had lain dormant for years, a group of artists got together to study this phase of the process. They wanted to see whether they could redeem Silk Screen from the purely commercial fate which had overtaken it.

The group, inspired by Anthony Velonis, approached the

WPA of New York City with a request for permission to create a silk screen art project. When permission was granted, they began to experiment with this industrialized graphic art and were amply rewarded when they found heretofore undiscovered possibilities in it. They decided that here was a sensational new art "find" and backed up their experiments with original prints which made their way into exhibitions and thence to museums. Many newspapers and art journals gave this new art its well-deserved praise, and the artists gave the prints a new name. *Serigraphs*, as they called the silk screen prints, went on exhibition throughout the country, and from that time on artists everywhere began to talk about silk screen and realized its broad possibilities.

Fine silk screen prints were brought to the attention of the public through the efforts of Elizabeth McCausland, visionary art critic and writer. She arranged and sponsored exhibits that were a revelation to both critics and laymen. These fine art prints have also received the praise and endorsement of Carl Zigrosser, who as art critic and writer on graphic arts, arranged some of the early exhibitions at New York galleries.

In the brief existence of silk screen, almost every kind of subject and treatment has been essayed; some of the results have been blatant, some refined and subtle. Among the prominent artists who are lending distinction to the silk screen technique are Anthony Velonis, Harry Gottlieb, who exhibited the first one-man silk screen show at the ACA Gallery, Harry Sternberg, Elizabeth Olds, and a host of others. The roster is growing daily.

Specially noteworthy has been the work of the National Serigraph Society, New York, which has been the source of inspiration, clearing house, and temple of artists and print makers everywhere. The National Serigraph Society and its active director, Doris Meltzer, have been largely responsible for promoting this new print form and raising it to the level of a museum art form.

Thus runs the fabulous story of the discovery of silk screen as a fine art. Stenciling has been used by many people throughout the ages as a decorative art; lately its commercial possibilities have also been exploited, but once again the artistic is finding expression. The development of silk screen as a fine art will find more and more students and artists trying their hand at this new medium of expression. As more and more artists of prominence become identified with this process, good silk screen prints of unlimited pictorial range will be made available to the public.

(Note to 1983 printing: The National Serigraph Society is no longer in existence.)

Mallorca by Dorr Bothwell, 1951   *Metropolitan Museum of Art*

CHAPTER TWO

Basic Principles

Shio Rock, N. M. by Muse

National Serigraph Society

BASIC PRINCIPLES

THE silk screen process is based on the fundamental principle of the stencil. If paint or any other colored fluid is rubbed over a stencil, it will readily penetrate the unprotected portions and will be unable to pass through the masked portions.

Keeping this simple principle in mind, let us participate in an imaginary silk screen demonstration, so that we may appreciate how the principle works in practice. The stencil is affixed to a piece of silk that is stretched on a wooden frame. The silk acts as a screen support for keeping all the integral parts of the stencil in a fixed position, without any ties or other connecting links. This marks the outstanding difference between the silk screen and the common oilpaper and metal stencils.

Let us examine the stencil principle a little more closely. Silk, like other woven fabrics, is porous. The finer the weave or mesh, that is, the closer the strand fibers are to each other, the less porous the material; and inversely, the coarser the mesh, the more porous the fabric. For example, cheesecloth is exceedingly porous, but the fine bolting cloth used for silk screen is porous to a lesser degree. If we were to pour free-flowing paint into the silk-covered frame, we should find that the paint would gradually seep through the silk screen. To accelerate the penetration, we might agitate or rub the paint across the surface of the silk with a straight-edged cardboard or a squeegee, a rubber sweeper similar to a window washer. This would cause the paint to pass through the silk instantly.

As it would be difficult to handle loose silk, we stretch and tack the silk tightly on a rectangular wooden frame. This frame performs a double duty. It acts as a stretcher for the silk and also as a basin for a quantity of paint. Place a white card, smaller than the screen, on a flat table or drawing board. Rest the screen on top of this, so that the silk is in immediate contact with the card. Pour a little free-flowing red paint of a creamy consistency into the basin along one of the side banks. Starting at one side of the screen, scrape the squeegee across the silk to the opposite side. Raise the screen and behold! What was once a pure white card is now completely red. That simple motion of the squeegee pushing the paint across the screen has given the white card an allover coating of red paint. The mesh or fibers of the silk have in no way interfered with the complete penetration of color. The rubber squeegee has made the paint go through instantly and smoothly.

What paint there is in the basin may be enough to cover dozens of cards, as only a little paint is used up with each stroke of the squeegee. Let us continue with our demonstration.

We take a 1-inch square piece of thin paper and paste it to the underside of the silk, in the center of the screen. We rest the screen over a fresh white card as before and again squeegee red paint across. As we lift the screen this time, we find a solid red area interrupted by a white square. The paper square has served as a mask; the open silk corresponds to the printing area, the closed silk to the white area. This is known as *reverse printing*, where the desired design, the square, was stopped out to prevent the penetration of paint, and the surrounding area was left open. We have printed around the design. Of course, it doesn't matter whether the mask is a square, a circle, a meaningless geometric form, a letter of the alphabet, or a silhouette—whatever shape is blocked out on the screen will remain white on the print.

The next experiment almost suggests itself. We take a sheet of paper as large as the screen and cut a 1-inch square window out of the center of it. We discard the small paper cutout, and this time, we paste the large sheet to the underside of the screen. Again we print with red paint on a white card. Upon raising the screen this time, we observe that the resulting print is a 1-inch red square on a white ground. This is known as *direct printing*, where the desired design, the square, was left open for the penetration of paint, and the surrounding area was blocked out by the stencil. In this case, we have printed the design itself. Obviously, we have the same liberties in design that we had previously.

This demonstration has been kept simple to focus attention on the *principle* of the process rather than on the technique of stencilmaking. It might be well, as an epilogue to this demonstration and as a prologue to what is to follow, to state that there are five distinct ways of preparing a stencil. There are the paper, the block-out, the tusche, the film, and the photographic methods. Regardless of the method, the basic principle remains the same.

Flowers by Frank Davidson   *National Serigraph Society*

CHAPTER THREE

Basic Equipment

Ceramic Movements by J. Jay McVicker

National Serigraph Society

BASIC EQUIPMENT

THE fascination that silk screen holds for those who like to do their own color printing need not be dampened by a consideration of the complexity and cost of equipment; artists of modest means can afford it.

There are no bulky presses or dangerous machines; there is very little that can get out of order. A small unit need not weigh more than a few pounds and may be stored in the studio when not in use. It seems remarkable that such a simple and inexpensive portable printing unit can produce inexhaustible quantities of prints in black and white and in full color. The unit represents permanent equipment and does not demand an extravagant investment.

There is no limit to the size of a process printing unit. In commercial studios it is not unusual to see some screens that are large enough to reproduce gigantic displays and backgrounds 15 feet long. You can make a screen to fit the size of any reproduction you wish to make.

For purposes of clarification, we shall assume that we are interested in producing a picture of a given size, say 6 by 9 inches, the size of a page in this book. This assumption will

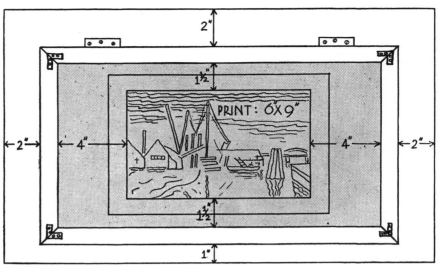

FIG. *a.*—*Relative dimensions of printing unit compared with size of print.*

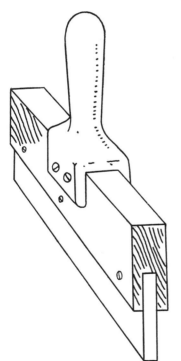

FIG. *b.*—*One-hand squeegee.*

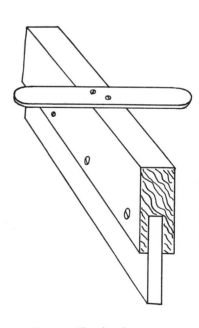

FIG. *c.*—*Two-hand squeegee.*

PLATE 2

make it possible to give specific construction details with definite size requirements for related materials. Dimensions can be varied to accommodate any size. The general proportions or relationship will remain the same, irrespective of any changes in dimensions.

Anyone with average dexterity in handling simple tools, anyone who is not "all thumbs," can easily construct a simple unit by following the specifications. Professional units can be purchased ready-made in many sizes.

The unit consists of a silk-covered wooden frame, a flat base or table, and a rubber squeegee.

THE FRAME

The function of the frame is to act as a supporting stretcher for the silk and also as a basin for the paint. Frames are usually rectangular. The frame should be constructed of well-seasoned wood, free from knots. It need not be any particular type of wood, but white pine furring strips, which are inexpensive and easily handled, are recommended. For our job, a frame of 9 by 17 inches inside dimensions can be made from a 6-foot strip $1\frac{1}{4}$ by 1 inch. This can be obtained from any local lumber dealer at about 4 cents a running foot.

The frame must be rigid, for a frame that is poorly constructed will, by twisting, distort the stencil and make multicolor registration impossible. Plate 3 offers several suggestions for joining corners in constructing the frame.

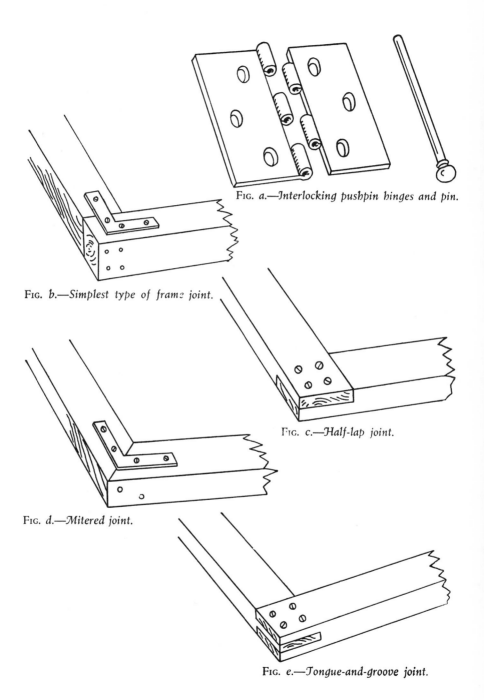

FIG. a.—Interlocking pushpin hinges and pin.

FIG. b.—Simplest type of frame joint.

FIG. c.—Half-lap joint.

FIG. d.—Mitered joint.

FIG. e.—Tongue-and-groove joint.

PLATE 3

Figure *b* shows the strips cut straight, nailed together, and reinforced on top with angle irons. This is the simplest type of frame construction. Figure *c* shows an interlocking type of frame with a half-lap joint. Figure *d* shows a mitered or picture frame corner. It is somewhat difficult to get perfect joining angles without the use of a miter box. Angle irons are again used for reinforcement. Figure *e* shows the tongue-and-groove type of frame corner, which is stronger than the first two and used professionally.

The finished frame should be sandpapered to remove any rough edges or protruding splinters. A frame with a smooth finish is generally easier to handle and offers a better surface for tacking the silk. A coat of shellac or lacquer on the raw wood will help prevent possible warping. This protective coat will also act as a *size* to keep paint from penetrating the fibers of the wood.

THE SCREEN FABRIC

There are a limited number of fabrics that can be used for the screen, such as silk bolting cloth, organdy, and copper mesh. Silk costs anywhere from $3.50 to $7.00 a yard, depending upon the quality and the size of the mesh, whereas organdy can be had for as little as 90 cents a yard. In spite of the difference in price, it is advisable to get silk. Silk fabric, commercially known as bolting cloth, will far outlast organdy and will produce sharper and cleaner prints. Organdy, not

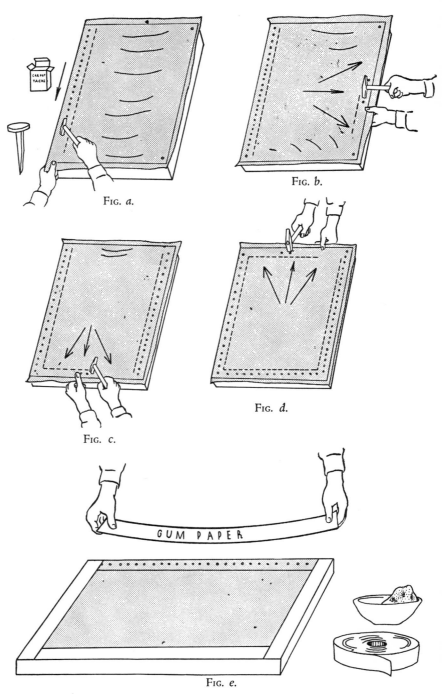

Fig. *a.*

Fig. *b.*

Fig. *c.*

Fig. *d.*

GUM PAPER

Fig. *e.*

Stretching the stencil fabric.

PLATE 4

having the elasticity or tensile strength of silk, becomes flabby with use. In view of the fact that the same silk screen can be used indefinitely, there is no real economy in the use of organdy, which has to be replaced frequently.

There is a domestic line of silk that sells for less than the silk imported from Japan or Switzerland. A good grade of silk, with interlocking meshes, does not shift during stretching, printing, or cleaning. Silk comes in widths of 40, 45, 50, and 54 inches and can be bought in any length. A half yard of silk (18 by 40) will be more than enough for our frame. This will allow enough grip for pulling the silk taut while stretching it on the frame. Bolting cloth is classified according to the mesh, which ranges from #4 to #20. Your dealer can supply you with a table showing the number of meshes to the linear inch and the corresponding number of the silk. The higher the number, the finer the mesh; the finer the mesh, the sharper the print. The #12 mesh silk is medium fine and is recommended for all-around work.

Stretching the screen fabric. As there is no right or wrong side to the silk, it doesn't matter how you hold it. Use #4 carpet tacks to fasten the silk to the frame. These may be bought at any hardware store or "five-and-ten."

To stretch the silk, place the frame on a sturdy table and center the silk over the frame. Drive a #4 carpet tack into each corner so that the silk will be temporarily held in place. Now stretch one side at a time, beginning with one of the long sides as in Plate 4, Fig. *a*. Grip the silk firmly, pulling it tight, and insert tacks all along the side about an inch apart. With this finished, start at the center of the opposite side, pull the silk, and insert tacks from the center toward the ends as seen in Fig. *b*.

Now that both long sides are tacked, start at either of the short sides, again pulling and inserting tacks as shown in Fig. *c*. The last side, if properly stretched, should take up any wrinkles, leaving the screen taut and firm. See Fig. *d*. The stretched silk on the frame results in a drumlike surface, resilient and alive.

Each time that you insert the tacks, be sure the heads of the tacks sink flush with the wood. The head as well as the shaft is necessary for holding the silk in place. Trim off the excess silk extending beyond the frame and cover the four rows of tacks with brown gummed paper (see Fig. *e*). Turn the frame, basin side up, and, folding the strips of gummed paper in half lengthwise, seal the four inside edges of the frame by pasting the paper strips so that half goes on the silk and half on the wood. This lining will help to hold the silk and will also prevent paint from oozing through the frame during printing. The gummed paper should be shellacked or lacquered to make it waterproof. You can extend the lacquer 1/2 inch or so into the screen on the long ends, and about 2 inches into the screen on each of the short sides. The printing is never done close to the frame, and so the 2 inches of lacquer on either side will serve admirably as banks for holding the paint during printing.

The method of stretching the silk as outlined here do⟨ represent the only way in which this can be success⟨.. accomplished. It is an expression of personal preference for a simple, orderly technique which has been found to bring good results.

THE BASE

The base is the flat board upon which the screen frame rests. One of the long sides of the frame is hinged to this base so that the frame may be easily raised and lowered. The base should be slightly larger than the frame. Allowing about 1 inch for the thickness of the wood, the outside dimensions of the frame should be 11 by 19 inches. To allow room for hinges and for a leg support at the side, the base should be about 13 by 24 inches.

Any flat board that will not warp easily can be used as the base. Even an old drawing board or artist's table top will do the trick. Whatever board is used, care should be taken to keep it clean and smooth. The smoothness of the board is of especial importance when printing on thin paper, because any protruding foreign matter on the base underneath the paper would cause a ruinous bump on the print.

Three guides are attached to the printing base to control registration. They may be made of paper, cardboard, fiber-

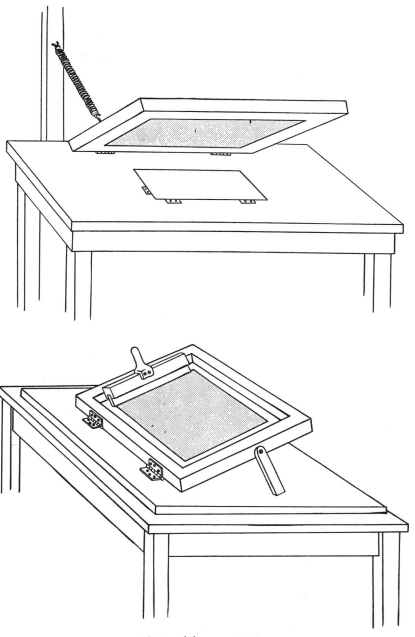

Types of frame supports.

PLATE 5

board, celluloid, or metal. Metal guides will not wear away regardless of the constant repetitive pressure to which they are subjected. Whatever kind is used, as determined by the job to be run, the guides should be fastened securely to the printing base so that they will not move during printing. One way to fix them tight is to nail or tack them to the base. This, however, leaves holes in the base when the guides are removed, and if these holes are multiplied for each job, it doesn't take long to ruin the base. Perhaps the best plan is to glue or rubber-cement the guides to the base, so that when they are removed they will leave the base unimpaired.

Register guides vary with the size of the card to be printed. They should be equal in thickness or slightly thinner than the card. If the guides are heavier than the card, they will cause ridges in the screen and will interfere with good printing contact. To facilitate registration, it may be found helpful to use guides of a color different from the printing stock.

HINGES

Two sets of 2½- or 3-inch pushpin hinges are needed for the stencil unit. A set consists of two interlocking hinges, male and female, held together by a sturdy shaft or pin. The pin can be pulled out at will to release one hinge from the other. To attach the hinges, the frame is centered on the base with the silk side down. Use 3/4-inch flat-headed screws to fasten the hinges. One male and one female hinge are attached at each end of the long side of the frame, and the mates of these hinges are attached similarly to the base (see Plate 5). The frame can now be raised and lowered like a horizontal door, and it will always fall back in exactly the same position.

If an artist has several frames, it is a good idea to space the hinges on all the frames equally, so that any frame used can be placed on the same printing bed without shifting the hinges to match. The base thus becomes the master printing bed for any number of frames with matched hinges.

Check the hinges occasionally to see that the screws have not become loose, for loose hinges will play havoc with the registration of multicolor prints.

LEG STAND

Various devices are used to hold up the screen. Commercial printers employ counterbalances in the form of projecting bars. These bars are weighted down to raise the screen as soon as the printer takes his hand from the screen. Some prefer overhead pulleys extending from the ceiling to the frame. But the artist need not go into that problem so seriously. The simplest way is to attach a leg stand or drop stick to the side of the frame, as seen in Plate 5, Fig. b. This stick, about 1 foot long, drops down by its own weight to a perpendicular position when the frame is raised. An old metal support such as is used to prop up the lid of a phonograph, or a door spring as shown in Fig. a, may be used.

THE SQUEEGEE

The squeegee is the tool employed to push the paint through the silk screen and deposit it on the card underneath. Each scrape from one side of the screen to another results in an impression.

There are two types of squeegees: the grip-handle type, or one-hand squeegee; and the two-hand squeegee. The latter type is operated by gripping the casing with both hands and pushing it across the screen. Study Plate 2, Figs. b and c.

It is important to fit the squeegee to the width of the frame. For our job, use an 8-inch squeegee, allowing a 1/2-inch sideplay.

The squeegee is made of thick rubber, $2\frac{1}{2}$ inches wide, sandwiched between a plywood casing, with the rubber blade protruding $1\frac{1}{4}$ inches beyond the casing. The blade is firm but flexible and peculiarly responsive to pressure. The squeegee costs about 20 cents a linear inch; the special grip handle, if desired, costs about 75 cents extra. The practicing artist should, at first, buy a squeegee that is ready-made. This may then be used as a model for constructing other squeegees.

After many prints, the edge of the rubber dulls, but it can be sharpened easily by stroking it over a long sandpaper board or abrasive garnet cloth several times.

The squeegee rubber should be kept sharp and square at the point where it contacts the screen. A sharp squeegee will mean sharper and cleaner prints. If well cleaned after each

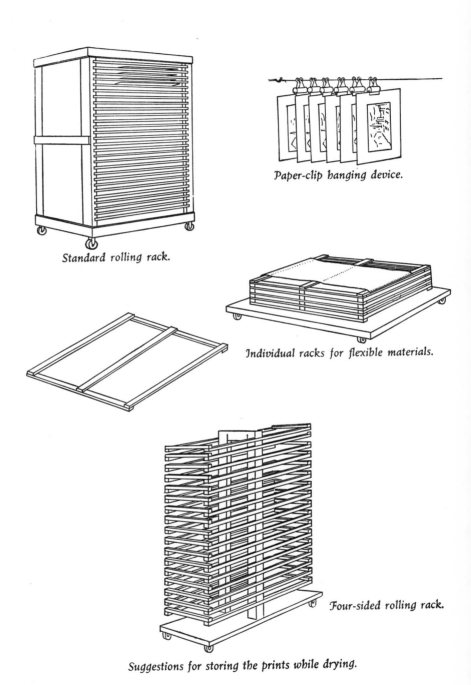

Standard rolling rack.

Paper-clip hanging device.

Individual racks for flexible materials.

Four-sided rolling rack.

Suggestions for storing the prints while drying.

PLATE 6

printing, a squeegee is a permanent, imperishable tool. Caked-up paint left on the squeegee, however, will rot and crack the rubber.

THE RACKS

The drying time of prints varies with the type and mixture of the paint used, the surface upon which the printing is done, climatic conditions, and the thickness of the paint deposit on the print. As yet, there is available no practical silk screen paint that dries so quickly as to allow prints to be safely stacked on top of each other as they are removed from the printing base. The time of drying may range from 10 minutes to 6 hours, and it therefore becomes necessary to devise some means of storing wet prints individually until they are dry enough for further handling.

If you plan a small edition of 50 prints, let us say, they can be distributed on tables, chairs, etc. The situation becomes less manageable as the edition runs into hundreds or perhaps thousands. The simplest way to handle a fairly large quantity of wet prints made on paper, lightweight cardboard, etc., is to clip each individual print to a strong wire line with paper clips, as shown in Plate 6. This is the same system that is used by photographers to dry wet negatives. As the prints set, the earlier prints may be brought closer together on the wire to allow room for later prints. Plate 6 shows professionally made racks that are in use in many studios.

Muse

Morning Fog by Muse

Night Watcher by Janet Turner, 1955   *National Serigraph Society*

CHAPTER FOUR

The Paper Stencil Method

Dark Wings by Sylvia Wald, 1954

THE PAPER STENCIL
METHOD

To simpify matters in the chapters that follow, we have taken certain facts for granted and now pause to elaborate on these facts, hoping thus to establish a common ground of information.

The silk screen artist will find that he has a wide choice of different stencil techniques, his choice depending upon the nature of the work to be reproduced. Prints are frequently made in which one or more of the methods are combined. Silk screen stencils do not print in reverse; the design on the stencil and the printed design both face in the same direction. No allowances for reversal need be made on the stencil.

Our instructions for each stencil method are based on the assumption that the artist is fully equipped, except for the new materials to be used. We shall list all the required materials, but to avoid monotonous repetition, any materials and procedures shared in common by more than one stencil-making method will be described in detail only the first time we come across them.

We have previously agreed to make a 6- by 9-inch print. This means that our original as well as the card to be printed, allowing a 1-inch margin all around, measures 8 by 11 inches. The frame, the inside dimensions of which are 9 by 17 inches, with the silk properly stretched, is hinged to a smooth base about 13 by 24 inches, and a pliable 8-inch rubber squeegee is available for forcing color through the screen. We shall limit ourselves to the use of process oil paints for printing, and the subject of printing will be covered in a separate chapter. In other words, every stencil technique will be described up to the point where the stencil is ready for printing.

In this discussion of stencils, it might be more confusing than instructive to go into the question of printing multicolor designs. For this reason, the procedure for making stencils as outlined in the following five chapters applies only to single-color designs. Chapter Nine will deal exclusively with the special problems and techniques of multicolor reproductions.

Making paper stencils corresponds so closely to the artist's experience in frisket making that he should find the transition a natural one. The paper stencil is nothing more than a cut paper mask pasted to the silk. Paint squeegeed across the screen will penetrate the open areas of the mask, which correspond to the shape of the design. The cost of stencil paper is almost negligible. The stencils are easy to cut and easy to remove from the screen when the printing is finished.

Paint can be applied more generously with this type of stencil than with any other. Artists who like heavy daubs of paint will find the paper stencil sympathetic to their technique.

This stencil should be reserved for large area work of simple designs.

MATERIALS

1. *Stencil paper*. This is the paper from which the stencil is made. Any thin white bond paper or the type of paper commonly used by sign painters for window streamers can be used. It should lie flat, be transparent, and somewhat absorbent. Tracing paper is not absorbent enough. If the stencil paper is not sufficiently transparent for you to see through it clearly, rub it with kerosene or turpentine. Stencil paper can be bought in flat sheets or rolls and is available at art-supply stores.

2. *Stencil knife*. This knife is used for cutting the stencil paper. It has a blade made of tempered steel with an oblique cutting edge. There are various shaped blades, but the *hatchet* type X-Acto blade is best for our purposes. Some knives come with detachable blades, and there is also a swivel knife, which, though ingenious, is not very practical because it cannot be guided as easily as a fixed blade. Do not use the stencil knife as a general utility tool for cutting cardboard, prying thumbtacks loose, etc. This small but sturdy knife, used only for its intended purpose, will last indefinitely, needing only an occasional sharpening.

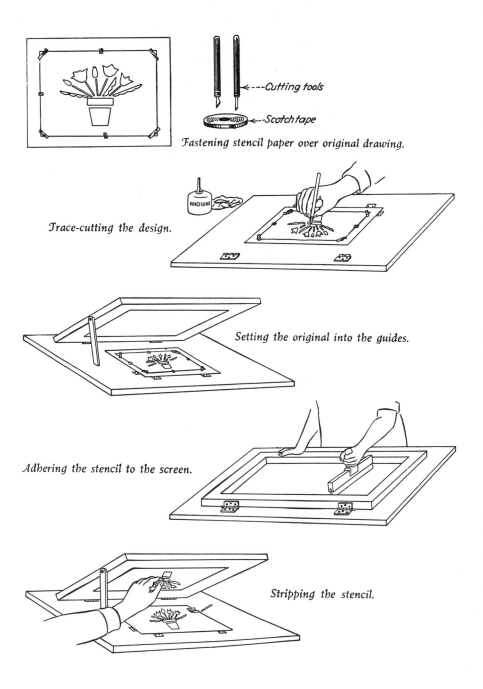

Fastening stencil paper over original drawing.

Cutting tools

Scotch tape

KEROSENE

Trace-cutting the design.

Setting the original into the guides.

Adhering the stencil to the screen.

Stripping the stencil.

44

PLATE 7

3. *Sharpening stone.* There are two types of sharpening stones, one requiring oil as a lubricant and the other, water. It makes no difference which one you use; both do the job equally well. A reversible carborundum stone, coarser on one side, may also be used. The sharpening stone is used in the following way: Hold the entire knifeblade flat against the stone with the sharp edge facing right. Draw the blade across the stone from right to left. Turn the blade so that the sharp edge faces left and draw the knife across from left to right. Sharpen the entire cutting edge, not just the point. A few strokes in both directions ought to be enough to keep the blade in tune for a while.

4. *Scotch tape.* Some artists find Scotch or masking tape indispensable and prefer it to thumbtacks for it does not injure the surface that it contacts. It holds fast and yet can be removed easily. The same piece may be used more than once.

PROCEDURE (Refer to Plate 7)

1. Raise the screen. Center the original drawing on the printing base. The long sides of the original should always run parallel to the long side of the base, as seen in Plate 5, Fig. *a.*

2. Disengage the screen. To release the screen from the base, slip the pushpins from the hinges. You will work more

comfortably if you temporarily remove the screen than if you keep it raised over the base.

3. Set the registry guides. Three guides are used to register the cards on the printing base. Two 1-inch guides are placed snugly against the lower edge of the card, each about 1/2 inch away from the end of the card. The third guide is usually placed about 1 inch up along the left side of the card. If the card is 1/16 inch thick, the guides should be 1/16 inch thick or less. For an edition not exceeding several hundred copies, small strips of cardboard cut to size and rubber-cemented down to the base serve admirably. For editions running into thousands, metal or celluloid guides are needed to withstand greater wear and tear. These guides can be rubber-cemented, glued, or nailed to the base. Make sure the original art is snug against the three guides.

4. Fasten the stencil paper over the original. Cut a sheet of paper, about 9 by 17 inches, to fit the area of the screen. Center it over the original and fasten it down securely at each corner with small pieces of Scotch tape. Make certain that the paper lies flat on the drawing.

5. Trace-cut the design. Use the knife to trace the complete outline of your design onto the transparent paper. Hold the stencil knife as you do a pencil, but a bit more perpendicular. Do not bear too heavily on the tool. Apply just

enough pressure to cut through the paper without digging into the original. A little experience will guide you in this matter. Leave all parts of the cut stencil intact. If you are afraid of ruining the original by digging into it, make a tracing of it and transfer it to a cardboard the same size as the original, using it as the master sketch.

6. Mark the areas to be stripped. Designate with an X or some other symbol those parts of the paper corresponding to the areas on your design to be printed. This will guide you later in stripping the right parts of the stencil.

7. Replace the screen in the hinges. Be careful not to disturb the cut parts of the stencil. Push the pins all the way in to be sure that there is no play in the hinges.

8. Remove the Scotch tape. The tape must be removed from the stencil paper cautiously so that the paper will not shift from its position on the original. The tape is removed so that the stencil, paper may be released from the original when it is transferred to the screen.

9. Lower the screen. For good adhesion, the silk of the screen should be in perfect contact with the stencil paper.

10. Adhere the screen. The paint is the only adhering agent used for affixing the stencil to the silk screen and must

therefore be of a rather heavy consistency. Paint that is too thin will not hold the paper stencil to the screen. Pour the paint along one of the banks of the screen and apply even pressure on the squeegee as you pass it across the screen. There is no fear of getting paint marks on the original, for as yet there are no open areas on the stencil through which paint might pass.

11. Raise the screen. Lift the screen and rest it on the side stick or leg stand. Be sure that the frame is not raised so high as to throw over paint and squeegee. You will note that the entire sheet of stencil paper, with all its parts, is adhered flat to the underside of the silk.

12. Strip the stencil. Peel off all parts of the stencil bearing the stripping symbol. This will leave part of the silk open, through which paint will pass.

13. Remove the original from the base. The drawing has served its purpose and may be removed from the guides. The stencil is now ready for printing.

The paper stencil deposits a heavy layer of paint; the thicker the paper used, the thicker the deposit of paint. Where the consumption of paint is not an important consideration, and this is likely in limited editions, the artist can experiment with interesting heavy impasto effects.

The life of the stencil is limited to fewer than 500 impressions, because the paint begins to ooze through when the stencil paper becomes saturated and heavily burdened with accumulated paint. The paper stencil can be used with any type of printing medium except tempera colors, for the water in the tempera color will wrinkle the paper and make sharp printing impossible. If the pressure of the squeegee causes any small isolated centers to shift, apply some glue, shellac, or lacquer to the silk directly over these parts. These mediums, seeping through the silk, will hold the centers firmly to the silk. It is not possible to store this stencil for future use, as the paper comes off when the screen is cleaned.

When you plan to use the paper stencil for reproducing your drawing, choose only subjects that can be rendered in keeping with the technical limitations of this method. Avoid crosshatching, stippling, and delicate contour drawing. Consider what to leave out as much as what to put in. This restriction may be looked upon as an advantage. By eliminating unnecessary details, paper stencil reproductions are characterized by a direct, simple, and bold quality.

REMOVING THE STENCIL

At the end of the run, when the paint remaining in the screen has been scooped up as described on page 171, raise the screen and merely peel off the paper from the mesh of the silk. This will come off without any trouble, as the paper is held to the silk only by the adhesive property of the paint.

Then wash the screen with a solvent compatible with the type of paint used. (Refer to the table on page 179.) Be sure that no paint or solvent remains in the silk. Those centers that required special adhesion should also be washed out with their proper solvents.

Dogwood by Riva Helfond

CHAPTER FIVE

The Block-out Stencil Method

Con Barrios by Zulema Damianovich

THE BLOCK-OUT
STENCIL METHOD

THE block-out method does not call for extraordinary equipment or new tools. The stencil is formed by simply blocking or masking out portions of the silk screen with a liquid such as glue, shellac, or lacquer and leaving the silk untouched where the paint is to go through. These masking mediums share the common property of drying hard in a short time. The screen is thus covered in part with an impenetrable coating, which restricts the flow of paint to confined areas. The block-out medium, therefore, really forms the substance of the stencil, and serves a purpose similar to that of the paper mask described in Chapter Four.

The choice of block-out medium will depend upon certain conditions. If you are planning to print with water colors, for example, it would be folly to use glue, a water-soluble substance, to block out the screen. Lacquer or shellac, water-resisting mediums, should be used instead. On the other hand, when the paint to be used is not soluble in water, it is all right to choose glue as the masking medium, as the stencil will then be easily dissolved in water when no longer needed.

There are two principal ways of making a block-out stencil. The simpler way is to brush in the glue, lacquer, or shellac directly on the silk. Another way, a bit more involved, is first to *size* the silk with a filler to provide a smoother working surface for painting in the stencil. Since each method has its place and advantages, both will be described in detail to give the artist an opportunity to experiment with each.

WORKING ON THE UNSIZED SILK
MATERIALS

1. *Block-out liquids.* Glue, lacquer, or shellac may be used as stopping-out mediums. Glue as it is bought is usually too heavy to work with; it should be thinned with water to a consistency compatible with easy brushing. If you find it difficult to work with glue that appears colorless when applied to the silk, a staining solution such as water dye, ink, or water color may be used to tint the glue. Your work on the silk can thus be made visible in contrast with the white screen. The coloring matter is inert and is used only to enable the artist to see what he is doing.

If the lacquer is too heavy to work with, add a little lacquer thinner to it. Lacquer is obtainable in colors and therefore does not require any added coloring matter to increase its visibility. The intense color of black lacquer makes a good contrast to the white silk. Lacquer stencils can be used with any type of paint except silk screen printing lacquers.

Orange shellac is thinned with denatured alcohol if it is too heavy. It is not used popularly as it is difficult to remove from the screen. The shellac seems to become impregnated in the mesh of the silk and requires vigorous scrubbing with alcohol to dissolve stubborn traces.

2. *Brush.* Any artist's or lettering brush that you are accustomed to work with will do. As in painting, use a small brush for detail work and a large brush for broader areas. The brush should be washed with the appropriate solvent soon after use (see table on page 179).

PROCEDURE (Refer to Plate 8)

1. Raise the screen. Center the original on the base and set the registry guides.

2. Lower the screen. The original should be visible through the silk.

3. Trace the drawing. Make a key tracing of the original with a pencil, or pen and ink onto the silk. Trace carefully every line and shape of the drawing, which is seen through the silk. When this is finished, you have a complete picture outline to serve as a guide for your work with the brush.

4. Prop up the screen. Raise the screen slightly with a block of wood or other prop, so that the silk does not touch the drawing underneath.

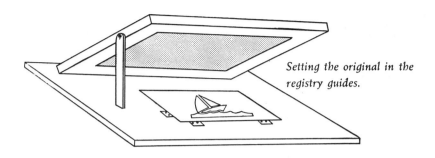

Setting the original in the registry guides.

Tracing the drawing on the silk.

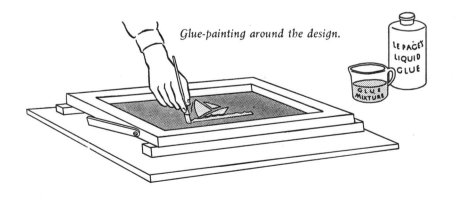

Glue-painting around the design.

PLATE 8

5. Remove the original from the base. As the silk carries a complete tracing of the drawing, the original may be removed from the base.

6. Brush in the screen. Brush in with glue, lacquer, or shellac those parts of the tracing that are to stop out the paint. These parts will form the *closed* areas of the stencil. The parts left untouched will form the *open* stencil, through which paint will flow.

7. Allow the glue to dry. Glue will dry within 1 hour. Lacquer will dry within 15 minutes. Shellac will dry within 1/2 hour. Refrain from impatiently touching the tips of your fingers to the screen to see whether it is still tacky. If it is, your fingerprints will leave pinholes showing the point of contact. As there is no danger of overdrying, give it plenty of time.

8. Check the screen. When the stencil is dry, hold it up against the light to check for pinholes. It may be necessary to retouch certain areas that haven't been completely stopped out. Touch up such leaks with the same liquid used to make the stencil. The stencil is now ready for printing.

Glue shows a surprising power of withstanding the constant scraping pressure of the squeegee, and glue stencils may last for innumerable impressions. After several thousand prints, however, the masking glue tends to break down in the form of tiny pinholes. If these pinholes are stopped out, the life of the stencil is extended. Lacquer and shellac stencils will withstand longer wear before they require this "doctoring." At the completion of printing, after the paint has been cleaned from the screen, the block-out stencil may be stored for any period of time for future use.

The block-out stencil makes possible techniques such as stippling and dry brush effects that are not practical with the paper stencil. It must be remembered that the work on the silk represents a negative plate of the print. In other words, you paint *around* the design, leaving the design itself open.

DISSOLVING THE STENCIL

To dissolve a glue stencil, wash both the top and bottom sides of the silk with warm or cold water. This will melt away the glue and leave the screen serviceable again for new work. Glue washes out more easily than lacquer or shellac. Water, the solvent for glue, can be used freely, but lacquer thinner and alcohol, which are required for the other stencils, cost from $1 to $1.50 a gallon. Be sure to dry the screen thoroughly before putting it away.

WORKING ON THE SIZED SCREEN

A sized screen is used only for lacquer or shellac stencils, because the glue sizing, which is applied on the silk before the masking medium, makes it possible to remove this medium merely by dissolving the glue sizing with water. What is more, a sized lacquer or-shellac stencil produces sharper prints than those stencils made by brushing the lacquer or shellac directly onto the raw silk.

MATERIALS

1. *Le Page's glue*. The glue is used as a sizing for the screen. It is diluted in water, about 1 part of glue to 3 parts of water. The glue leaves a thin but durable deposit on the screen.

2. *Lacquer or shellac*. The same lacquer or shellac is used as with the unsized block-out stencil.

PROCEDURE (Refer to Plate 9)

1. Raise the screen. The procedure for setting the original in the guides is the same as before.

2. Disengage the screen. Remove the pins from the hinges and take the screen off the base. Prop it up on a flat table, screen basin up. You may keep the screen in its hinges, if you raise it up high enough so that the silk doesn't touch the bed below.

3. Size in the silk. Pour a little of the diluted glue along one bank of the screen. Using a stiff piece of cardboard with a clean sharp edge, scrape the glue-sizing mixture across the

Glue-sizing the screen.

LE PAGE'S LIQUID GLUE

GLUE SOLUTION

ALCOHOL

SHELLAC

Applying masking liquid around the design.

WATER

Washing out the sizing.

PLATE 9

silk. Scrape it several times if you feel you have not covered the entire silk, but try to get an even coating of glue.

4. Allow the sizing to dry. If you are in a hurry, use a fan to dry the sizing so that you may get to work sooner. There is no fear that the sizing will dry too long. When the screen is completely dry, reset it in the hinges.

5. Brush in the design. The sizing does not affect the natural transparency of the silk, and the drawing can be clearly discerned through the sized screen. A pencil tracing is not needed, because it is not possible for the lacquer or shellac to flow through the sizing to mar the original. Brush in the design with lacquer or shellac directly on the glued-in silk.

6. Inspect the screen. Be sure to touch up any pinholes or leaks.

7. Prop up the screen. Disengage the screen and prop it up with two blocks so that the silk does not come in contact with the table. Do not tilt it or set it at an angle, as it is essential that the screen lie flat.

8. Dissolve the glue sizing. When the masking medium is perfectly dry, it is safe to wash out the exposed sizing. Keeping the screen level, wash the *top* of the silk with a wet

sponge. The water doesn't affect the lacquer or shellac but quickly melts the glue sizing wherever the glue is exposed. Care must be exercised not to tip the screen at an angle while dissolving the sizing. Do not use so much water that it will flood the underside of the silk and run into the areas directly underneath the lacquer or shellac. This would loosen the foundation upon which the lacquer or shellac rests and destroy the stencil. Remember that the water sponge is applied only to the side of the silk that bears the masking medium.

9. Dry the screen. Using a cloth pad, vigorously wipe out all traces of melted sizing from the open mesh. Again, do not touch the underside of the silk. When the sizing is completely removed, the stencil is open where the paint is to go through.

10. Reengage the screen in the hinges. Insert the pushpins all the way in, and the screen is ready for printing.

The sized screen will last for large editions of prints, it may be preserved for future use, and it produces somewhat sharper lines than the unsized screen. This screen is as easily cleaned as an ordinary glue screen; yet because lacquer and shellac may freely be used as masking mediums, the screen is good for printing with tempera colors in limited editions. The water content in the tempera colors will eventually work its way into the underside of the silk and etch into the lacquer by dissolving the sizing. This type of screen may be used indefinitely for printing with waterproof process oil colors.

Landscape by Doris Meltzer.
A good example of what can be achieved by combining glue block-out stencils with the tusche method. Printed in eight colors. *Size of print 14 by 19 inches.*

PLATE 10   63

DISSOLVING THE SIZED STENCIL

To dissolve this stencil, rub both sides of the screen with a water-soaked sponge. This time use plenty of water, especially on the *underside* of the screen. This will dissolve all the glue sizing underneath the lacquer or shellac, which, in turn, will cause the lacquer and shellac to scale off and clear the silk.

Fossils of Pompeii by Leonard Pytlak   *Metropolitan Museum of Art*

CHAPTER SIX

The Tusche Stencil
Method

Bridge of Carquinez Straights by W. Colescott

THE TUSCHE STENCIL METHOD

HE tusche stencil is by far the most practical and adaptable for fine-art printing. It has unlimited possibilities. The tusche stencil works on the principle of the chemical resistance of a greasy substance, such as lithographic tusche, to glue, which is water-soluble. When an area of the silk screen is painted with tusche, and the whole screen is then coated with glue, the tusched-in area will act as a stopping-out medium for the glue. When the tusche is later dissolved, the glue that covered it scales off and breaks away, leaving an unobstructed area on the silk. This is the open area of the screen, ready to receive the paint.

With the exception of the photographic method, the tusche technique most closely approximates the freedom of the original drawing, reproducing the spontaneity of the artist's design. Every tusche stroke on the silk is a latent paint stroke in the finished print.

Whereas in some stencil methods described in this book the artist has to get accustomed to working *around* his design, the tusche method requires no such orientation or acquisition of new skills. The tusche, an intense black in color, contrasting sharply against the dull whiteness of the silk, makes the artist's work clearly discernible on the silk and is, in effect, a preview of the print. With tusche stencils, you may work from a finished drawing or from preliminary roughs. It is a method that may be compared to lithography in its wide range of techniques, textures, and special effects.

Tusche stencils, like block-out stencils, may be prepared either on the raw silk or on a sized screen. Because of the mesh of the silk, prints made with this stencil show a slightly rough texture around the edges. This burr, or sawtooth edge, may be reduced to a minimum if the screen upon which the tusche is applied is first sized. The artist will have to decide for himself whether or not he wants to retain that burr before selecting his stencil.

WORKING ON THE UNSIZED SCREEN
MATERIALS

1. *Lithographic tusche. a.* Korn's liquid tusche. This is a slightly greasy black fluid resembling India ink. Shake the bottle thoroughly before using to stir up the tusche sediment that may have settled on the bottom. The tusche is applied directly on the silk. If you should find the tusche so watery that it drips through the mesh of the silk, you may apply one of these remedies: (1) Prop up the screen slightly so that the silk does not touch the master sketch. (2) Place a quantity of

tusche on a blotter, using the blotter as a palette and pool. After several minutes, the excess water will settle into the blotter, leaving a tusche of the right consistency on top. (3) In anticipation of using the tusche, keep the bottle open overnight to allow the excess moisture to evaporate.

If the tusche has gotten too heavy to flow easily, you can safely disregard the instructions on the label, which specify, "Use Distilled Water," for plain water is just as good for our purpose.

Tusche is never diluted with the expectancy of getting a variety of color tones. Tonal quality is attained during printing, not during stencil making.

b. Lithographic crayon. The crayon may be obtained in stick or pencil form. The stick is usually about 1/4 inch square and 2 inches long. The pencil tusche is a thin crayon around which black paper is tightly wound so that the crayon may be handled like a pencil. This paper is unwound in ribbons as the pencil is used. Lithographic crayons come in various grades from very soft to very hard.

2. Brush. No special type of brush is necessary. Use the brush to which you are accustomed. The tusche brush can be cleaned with water while the tusche is still wet, and with kerosene or turpentine when the tusche has dried.

3. Glue. The glue should be free flowing and of the consistency of heavy cream. If it is too heavy, thin it with water. There is no practical way of fixing glue that is too thin.

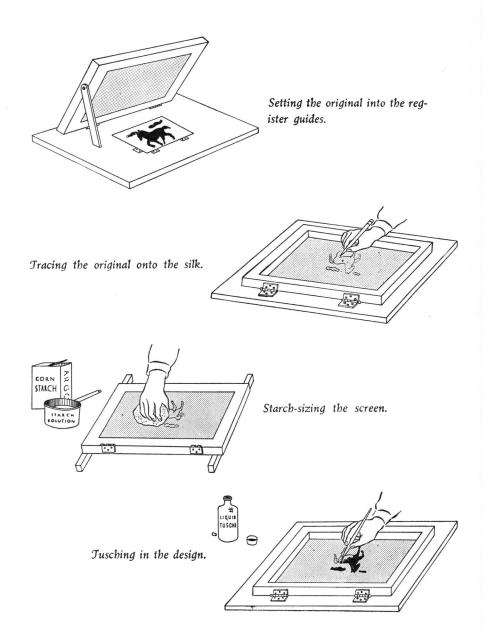

Setting the original into the register guides.

Tracing the original onto the silk.

Starch-sizing the screen.

Tusching in the design.

PLATE 11

4. *Kerosene*. Kerosene is used to dissolve the tusche. Use naphtha or benzine if you happen already to have those on your studio shelf. Kerosene, however, costs so little that it can be used generously, yet is just as good.

PROCEDURE (Refer to Plates 11 and 12)

1. Raise the screen. The procedure for setting the original in the guides is the same as before. If you are particularly proud of your original drawing and do not want to spot it with tusche that might seep through the silk, make an exact pencil tracing of it on a card the same size as the original and use this as the master sketch.

2. Lower the screen. Make an exact tusche facsimile of the drawing as it is seen through the silk. The silk presents a nice textured surface to work on with liquid tusche or lithographic crayon.

Any mistakes in making the stencil may be washed out with water while the tusche is wet, or with kerosene when the tusche has set. Use a pad of cotton or a rag folded over a finger.

3. Disengage the screen. Release the screen from the hinges and prop it up on two blocks so that the silk is away from the table. If you like, leave the screen in the hinges and just prop it up so that the silk is an inch or so off the bed.

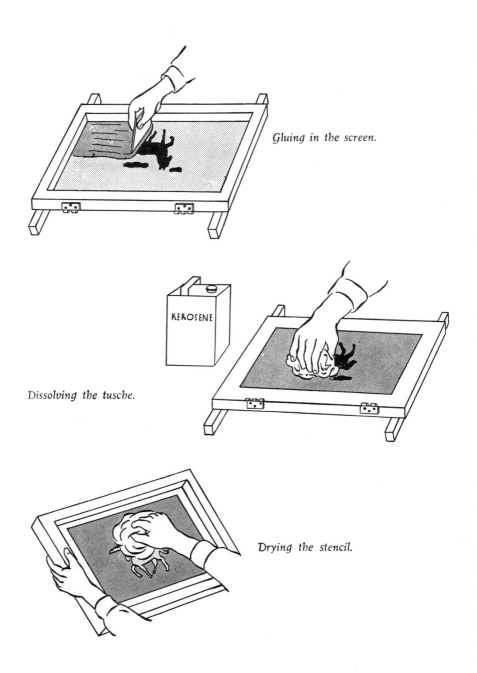

Gluing in the screen.

Dissolving the tusche.

Drying the stencil.

PLATE 12

4. Glue in the screen. Pour some glue along the bank of the screen. Using a stiff, sharp-edged cardboard, scrape the glue across the entire screen, including the tusched tracing. Wait a few minutes for the first coat to set and then make a return stroke. Get as even and smooth a coating as you can.

5. Allow the glue to dry. You may use an electric fan or small electric heater. There is no danger of the glue drying too long or too hard. If you are not in a hurry, you may leave the screen indefinitely to do other work.

6. Dissolve the tusche. Once the tusche has served its purpose of stopping out the glue in certain areas, wash it out. Rub both sides of the silk thoroughly with a kerosene-soaked rag. Concentrate mainly on the underside of the silk, particularly under the tusched areas. It is a good idea when not pressed for time to place kerosene-soaked newspapers or rags on the underside of the silk, allowing the kerosene to work into the tusche slowly. The longer it soaks, the more easily will the tusche wash off. As the tusche that served as a foundation for the glue comes off, the glue directly on top of it will also scale off and float away. You will note that the original blackness of the tusche becomes dimmer and fainter, until it disappears entirely. This indicates that the tusche is completely dissolved.

Boat Pier by Max Arthur Cohn. Size of print 12 by 18 inches. The print is true in treatment and effect to the original water color. The accidental white of the paper showing through the colored areas, and the extreme transparency of the tones, help to recreate the spirit of the aquarelle.

PLATE 13

7. Dry the stencil. Wipe up the kerosene, using fresh dry rags as needed, until the screen is perfectly dry.

8. Check the stencil. See that all the tusched areas are washed out. It may be necessary to scrape some of the stubborn edges gently with a fingernail or with a flexible suede brush. Also check for pinholes, which, if they appear, can be touched up and allowed to dry.

9. Replace screen in the hinges. The stencil is now ready for printing.

Prints made with the unsized stencil are characterized by a softness revealing the mesh mark of the silk along the edges. The tusche-glue stencil will last as long as the regular block-out stencil made with glue. It may be said that the heavier the coat of glue, the longer the life of the stencil. The coat of glue, however, must not be so heavy as to bury the tusche or so deep as to make it difficult to dissolve it. This stencil can be stored for future reprinting after the screen has been cleaned.

DISSOLVING THE STENCIL

If you are certain you won't ever want the stencil again, you may clear the silk for a new stencil. The tusche-glue stencil is easily dissolved in cold or warm water generously applied to both sides of the silk with a sponge or rags. The

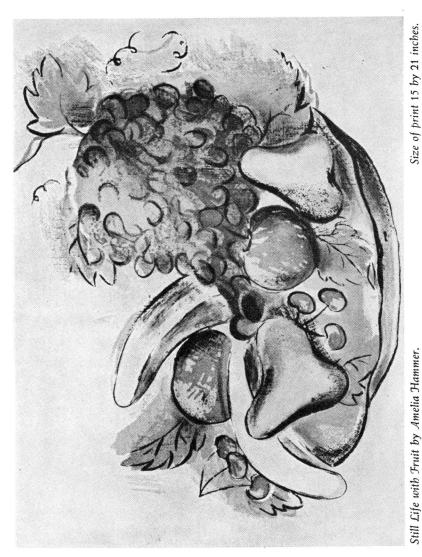

Still Life with Fruit by Amelia Hammer. *Size of print 15 by 21 inches.*
This is an exquisitely colored print made with twenty-four transparent colors. The artist succeeded very well in her endeavor to retain the delicacy of the original painting

PLATE 14

stencil should be thoroughly dried to make sure that the silk is left clear and free from any sign of glue.

WORKING ON A SIZED SCREEN

Where a sharper line technique is desired without sacrificing the spontaneity of the tusche stencil, the screen is sized, so that the spaces within the mesh of the silk are spanned by a filler. This provides a smoother, uninterrupted stroke, resulting in a finer line. This is especially desirable in fine contour line drawings, crosshatching, or fine lettering and intricate detail that may be tusched on the screen with a small brush, ruling pen, or ink compass.

MATERIALS

1. *Starch sizing.* This is plain grocery cornstarch diluted in warm or cold water, a heaping tablespoonful to a glass. The starch should be mixed thoroughly, until the water turns a milky white.

2. *Brush.*

3. *Lithographic tusche.*

4. *Glue.*

5. *Kerosene.*

PROCEDURE (Refer to Plates 11 and 12)

1. Raise the screen. The procedure for setting the original in the guides is the same as before.

2. Lower the screen. With the silk in contact with the drawing, make a key tracing in pencil or pen and ink directly on the silk, following all the lines of the original.

3. Remove the screen from the hinges. Disengage the screen and prop it up on a table so that the silk is not in contact with the table.

4. Size the screen. Using a sponge saturated with the starch solution, pass it across the silk several times, leaving as smooth a coat as possible. If you have used a pencil for the tracing, apply the starch to the underside of the silk so that the pencil lines will not wash off. If you have used India ink, the starch may be applied to either side of the silk. The waterproof ink will not dissolve.

5. Allow the sizing to dry. The sizing will dry normally in 1/2 hour. A moving current of air will hasten the drying. When the sizing is thoroughly dry, the screen will show a white chalky coating. The silk will have a smoother working surface.

6. Replace the screen in the hinges. The screen is now ready to receive the tusche. If it's more convenient, you may finish your tusche work before you replace the screen on the base.

7. Tusche in the design. As the starch sizing has not obliterated the tracing, you can clearly see just where to paint your design with the tusche. Apply the tusche as before.

8. Disengage the screen.

9. Glue in the screen.

10. Allow the glue to dry.

11. Dissolve the tusche. Dissolve the tusche as before. You need have no apprehensions about starch remaining in the open areas of the stencil. In the process of washing out the tusche, the starch has floated off.

12. Dry the stencil.

13. Check the stencil.

14. Replace the screen in the hinges.

Prints made with a sized stencil will be somewhat sharper and crisper than those made with the unsized stencil. Still finer work can be had with this type of stencil if the silk is of a finer mesh. Instead of a #12 mesh silk, a #14 or #16 should be used for extra-fine work. The stencils may be stored indefinitely for future use after the screens are cleaned of paint. With tusche you can reproduce work that is delicate and refined or bold and strong, as the subject requires.

Textural effects with tusche and litho crayon.

PLATE 15

Tusche-glue screens are good for printing with any medium such as oil color, enamels, lacquers, and other paints that are not water-soluble. If you have a special preference for tempera colors, the tusche-lacquer type of screen may be used. This works in the same way as the tusche-glue stencil, except that instead of glue, lacquer is spread over the tusche. When the tusche is dissolved, the lacquer will come off as readily as the glue.

DISSOLVING THE STENCIL

The sized tusche-glue stencil is dissolved with water in the same way as the unsized screen. The tusche-lacquer screen is dissolved with lacquer thinner.

TEXTURAL EFFECTS

Tusche may be used for any number of special textural effects. With the clever manipulation of an atomizer, airbrush, toothbrush, or comb, the solidity of liquid-tusche work may be softened in a variety of ways. Use the tusche on the screen just as you use paint or ink on paper for stippling, spattering, crosshatching, dry-brush effects, etc. The litho crayon used in combination with the liquid tusche on the same screen will shade off or soften the tusched-in areas. The soft sketchy line produced by the litho crayon may be accented with the liquid tusche to bring out high lights and depth, adding quality and character to the work.

Beach Scene at Sea Gate by Hyman Warsager. *Size of print 14 by 20 inches.* The pastel-like quality of this print is due to the sensitive treatment of the tusche crayon applied on the silk screen which was resting on an abrasive surface. Twenty-two colors were used in building up the design.

PLATE 16

Do not use too coarse a mesh for your screen; a #14 or #16 mesh silk will retain the desired texture of your work. To get a Ben Day or Ross board effect, place a piece of rough-grained Ross board or sandpaper under the screen so that the silk is in contact with the rough surface. Rub the litho crayon over the silk. A light rubbing will produce thin, isolated tusche dots, whereas a heavy application of the crayon on the silk will bring out the full depths of the minute valleys and hills created by the uneven surface underneath. Try a variety of surfaces. Experimentation with such diverse materials as canvas, leather, wire screens, end grain of wood, cloth, and Ross board should prove an interesting adventure and give full play to techniques.

Once the design is tusched in, the rest of the procedure for preparing the tusche stencil is the same as outlined before. Sometimes after gluing in the screen, when it is too late to do anything about it, you may discover that you cannot possibly dissolve the shaded areas. This is due to the fact that the litho crayon, when applied to the silk, was not pressed against it hard enough for the tiny particles to settle in the mesh of the silk. The tusche crayon should be applied so that it more than merely stains the silk; it should, no matter how soft the desired effect, to some extent impregnate the silk. To check the screen, hold it against the light before you glue it in to see how well the tusche has taken.

Just one more precaution: for very fine stippling or delicate

Side Street by Anthony Velonis. *Size of print 14 by 20 inches.*
The textural quality of this fine print shows the deft use of the tusche crayon. Printed in four colors.

PLATE **17**

shading, do not apply too heavy a coat of glue over the tusche or you may encounter some difficulty in dissolving the tusche that is buried beneath the heavy coat of glue. Precisely how heavy or thin the glue should be for this purpose cannot be stated objectively. Each artist will have to learn this for himself, just as he will develop other judgments through experimentation with the medium.

Forms #2 by Glenn Alps, 1952

Skyline by Harry Shokler   *National Serigraph Society*

CHAPTER SEVEN

The Film Stencil Method

After Hours by Ray Euffa

CHAPTER SEVEN

THE FILM STENCIL
METHOD

WHERE sharpness of line and preciseness of detail are essential to the quality of a print, the film method is suggested. The film stencil is made from a double-layered stopping-out film. The design is cut and stripped out of the top layer, and the rest of the film is adhered to the silk. When the underneath layer is peeled off, the silk is left open in the shape of the design originally cut from the film. Paint will pass freely through these unobstructed areas but will be stopped out by the remaining parts of the film stencil paper.

The stencil knife is not so yielding as a brush or pencil, but artists who have acquired manual dexterity in other processes involving metallic tools will soon get accustomed to the use and feel of the stencil knife.

Like the paper stencil method, this method is capable of reproducing designs with literally knife-cut sharpness; yet because of the flexible nature of the film, it is capable of infinitely greater detail. The crispness that distinguishes a print done with the film stencil has always been attractive to commercial printers. In fact, this is the method used for the greater part of all commercial process printing, as it is admirably suitable for clean lettering and sharp rendering of poster work.

MATERIALS

1. *Lacquer stencil film.* This is the film material from which stencils are cut. It is a transparent tissue made up of two layers: a thin sheet of lacquer supported on a sheet of glassine backing paper. This laminated film, which is sold as NuFilm, can be obtained in sheets 30 by 40 inches and also in rolls.

2. *Adhering thinner.* This is a volatile acetate liquid used to adhere the film stencil to the screen. It is put up in quart and gallon cans. Do not purchase it from just any painter's supply store but get it direct from the dealer who supplied you with the film. In this way you will be certain that it is the specific thinner for your film.

3. *Removing thinner.* This is a volatile acetate liquid used to dissolve the film stencil. Adhering thinner may also be used for this purpose, but being chemically less potent, the adhering thinner acts more slowly. Paint remover will also dissolve film stencils.

4. *Film stencil knife.* This is a simple cutting implement resembling a stylus, used to cut film stencils. It has a pencil-shaped handle, from which protrudes an obliquely cut thin blade of tempered steel about 1/8 inch wide and 3/4 inch long. Unlike the array of tools of various sizes and shapes used

in wood-block printing, no expensive assortment of cutting tools is required for the silk screen film technique. The same knife is used for cutting both broad and delicate work. There are several styles of stencil knives, with metal or wooden handles, but their function remains the same. Some have fixed blades, some removable blades, and some swivel blades. The kind of handle is of little importance; it is the blade that counts. Do not use the swivel-type blade, as it is difficult to control.

Try to keep the blade in good working condition, for a sharp blade imparts a smooth penetrating stroke, making cutting a pleasurable experience.

5. *Soft flannel cloth.* Any soft absorbent rags free from lint may be used to adhere the stencil film to the silk screen.

6. *Clear fill-in lacquer.* This is a free-flowing lacquer used to close the open silk surrounding the adhered film. It is a quick-drying stopping-out medium and may be thinned with lacquer thinner.

7. *Gooseneck lamp.* This adjustable table lamp can be picked up at any hardware store. It is better than overhead light as it is concentrated and can be directed at will. A lamp of this sort is almost indispensable for the close work involved in film cutting.

PROCEDURE (Refer to Plates 18 and 19)

1. Raise the screen. Place the original on the printing base and set the guides as for the other methods.

91

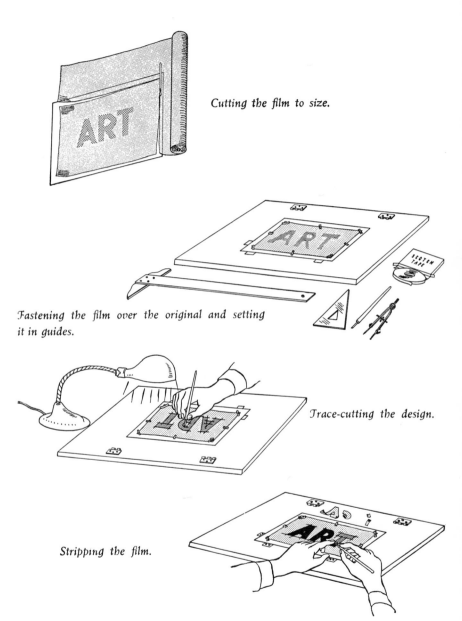

Cutting the film to size.

Fastening the film over the original and setting it in guides.

Trace-cutting the design.

Stripping the film.

PLATE 18

2. Disengage the screen from the base. If you remove the screen from the base, you can use the base as a drawing board on which to make the film stencil. Of course, once the guides are set, the screen may be left in the hinges and the original removed to a table more convenient for making the stencil.

3. Cut a sheet of film. The film should be larger than the area of the design to be reproduced. For our 6 by 9-inch print, a sheet of film 7 by 10 inches would be ample.

4. Center the film. Examine the film to distinguish the lacquer side from the glassine side. Center the film, lacquer side up, over the original.

5. Fasten the film to the original. Use plenty of Scotch tape to keep the film from shifting or bulging. You will note that the drawing is clearly discernible through the film.

6. Trace-cut the design. Trace-cut the complete outline of the design. The knife should be held lightly between the thumb and the index or the center finger. Hold it almost perpendicular to the film surface that you are cutting. Cut with a smooth, continuous movement, gripping the knife without tension to allow for facile tracing of straight and curved lines. Apply just enough pressure on the knife to cut through the lacquer skin without penetrating the supporting glassine back-

ing sheet. If you cut the film so deeply that the knife goes through the backing paper, the centers will fall out, thus defeating the purpose of the backing sheet.

It takes four cuts to make a line, regardless of its width or length. Intersect all lines that join to be sure that the areas they bind have been completely traced. These *overcuts* automatically close up when the film is adhered and do not show on the print.

You may trace-cut your work freehand or employ instruments where mechanical precision is desired. A metal-edged ruler or a celluloid triangle can be used as guides for cutting straight lines. A small bow compass rigged up with a cutting blade will cut mechanically perfect circles on the stencil film.

7. Strip the film. Strip the cut portions of the film that represent the areas to be printed. This is accomplished by carefully digging the point of the blade under the film from a corner of the incised area and then pulling the film up with the aid of a finger against the flat side of the blade. Don't nibble at the film. Try to strip out as large a piece as you can at one time to avoid wasteful motion.

8. Examine the film. The stripped parts exposing the glassine backing sheet represent the printing areas of the design. Examine these open areas and lightly brush off any stray particles of film or dust.

9. Remove the Scotch tape. Carefully remove most of the Scotch tape from the film, leaving only enough in strategic places to keep the film in place over the original.

10. Replace the screen. Make certain that the pushpins are all the way in. When you are sure that the original is registered in the guides, lower the screen so that the silk is in perfect contact with the film.

11. Adhere the stencil. Take a piece of soft cloth and fold it three or four times until it forms a pad. Saturate it with adhering thinner and use this cloth to adhere the film to the silk screen. Pass the rag swiftly across a small portion of the silk, being careful not to rub more than once or twice over any one area. Repeat this procedure instantly with a dry rag. Rub lightly at first to absorb excess thinner. As the lacquer thinner evaporates, you may rub more vigorously. There is little danger of rubbing too much with a dry cloth. You will note a slight change in the appearance of the film when it adheres to the silk. It's good practice to work on just a small area of film at a time, so that you'll have a chance to follow up immediately with the dry rag. Remember that a little thinner sparsely but evenly applied is all that it takes to adhere the film. Too much thinner will dissolve the film. If you have trouble adhering some spots, it may be due to lack of firm contact between the film and the silk. To remedy this situation, place

Adhering the stencil.

Stripping the backing sheet.

Stopping out the areas sur-rounding the stencil.

PLATE 19

a few heavy cards on the base directly under the stubborn areas to act as a "pack-up" for bringing the silk in closer contact with the film. Then give those spots a light going over with lacquer thinner and the dry rag.

12. Raise the screen. When you raise the screen, you will note that the film has come up with it. It has been pulled away from the original and is firmly adhered to the silk. Allow the adhesion to "set" for at least five minutes.

13. Strip the backing sheet. Start at any convenient corner and slowly peel the glassine paper. The film stencil remains intact on the screen.

14. Stop out the surrounding area. Before going ahead with the printing, all open areas of silk surrounding the film stencil should be stopped out in either of the following ways:

  a. For short runs, cut a sheet of flat absorbent paper to act as a mask surrounding the film. This should be attached to the underside of the screen. The natural viscosity of paint will make this paper mask cling to the silk just as in the ordinary paper stencil.
  b. For longer runs, scrape some fill-in lacquer over the silk all around the film with a stiff, sharp-edged cardboard. This may be done on the upperside or underside of the silk. Two coats usually assure leakproof coverage.

Street Scene by Von Arenburg.　　　　　*Size of print 6 by 9 inches.*
This print was screened with film stencils. Eight opaque colors were screened directly
on a dark gray stock. Over three thousand prints were made with the same stencils.

　　　　　　　　　　　　　　　PLATE 20

If the sheet of film used for the stencil is large enough to cover the screen, no special stopping-out medium is required. The stencil is now ready for printing.

The film stencil is practically imperishable; it can be used again and again for any number of reprints without showing signs of wear. This type of stencil can be used with many paints, except lacquer.

DISSOLVING THE STENCIL

To dissolve the film stencil, spread several layers of newspaper on the printing base. Saturate this newspaper bedding with removing thinner and lower the screen. Also spread some saturated newspapers on top of the silk and give the thinner time to work into the film from both sides. Then raise the screen, and you will find that the newspapers have attracted a good portion of the film. Those parts that did not come off can be dissolved by rubbing with a thinner-soaked rag until the screen is entirely cleared. Dry immediately with a large soft rag to wipe away any traces of lacquer thinner and dissolved film from the surface of the silk.

TEXTURAL EFFECTS

The film stencil technique is suitable for sharp lines and mass, rather than surface treatments or textural effects. Some effects are possible, but it is perhaps going beyond the means of this particular method to break up a surface for textural treatment. Here are some of the experiments you may try.

There are two techniques for getting a stippled effect. One way is to cut each little dot and strip the film in the regular manner. In this way, the size and shape of the dot are limited. The other way is to employ a pyrograph or electric burning needle. This is like a miniature soldering iron and comes with a set of tips of different sizes. The entire set costs less than $3 at any art-supplies store. The heated point, when set on the film, instantaneously dissolves the circle of film corresponding to the size of the tip. The heat dissolves only the lacquer, because it is not applied long enough to burn through the backing sheet. This is done before the stencil is adhered.

Remember that in the film method every line, regardless of how fine it is, has to be cut on all four sides in order to be stripped. Lines running in one direction can be stripped without much trouble, but intersecting lines break up the area into myriads of little boxes. Crosshatching, therefore, becomes a cumbersome and involved process. It can be done, but it is a tedious job to cut and strip such fine lines. To cut both sides of a fine line simultaneously, you can try a two-bladed instrument that is adjustable as to width. This can be made from a ruling pen, or a professional tool for cutting parallel lines may be purchased.

For a novel effect, perhaps a dusky cloud on a print, brush some lacquer thinner over the area in question on the film after the rest of the stencil has been cut and stripped. While the film is tacky from this application, press a piece of Ross board or sandpaper against it and lift it away instantly. The rough surface will take with it, as it is raised, lacquer dots corresponding to the size and pattern of the sandpaper. Other rough-grained materials, such as those used in obtaining similar effects with tusche, may also be tried. The film is then adhered in the regular way. This means of obtaining textural effects with a film stencil cannot easily be controlled.

Early Thaw by Hulda Robbins, 1956

Traps and Nets by Riva Helfond   *National Serigraph Society*

CHAPTER EIGHT

The Photographic Stencil Method

Hecatomb for Hector II by W. Colescott

THE PHOTOGRAPHIC
STENCIL METHOD

THE photographic principle has been applied to silk screen for a number of years, but not until recently has the process been perfected sufficiently to become as practical as the other methods described in this book. It does not require any special training in photography; it does not call for any involved or costly equipment. Fine pen and ink renderings can be reproduced in absolute facsimile, preserving every detail of the original.

The original sketch must either be drawn on a transparent tissue or photographed from the opaque original onto a transparent surface. The transparency becomes the *positive*. There are two ways of using this transparent positive for making a photo stencil. One is to expose the positive on a special sensitized tissue, which is later transferred to the screen. This is known as the *transfer* method. The other is to expose the positive directly on a sensitized screen. This is known as the *direct* method. Upon exposure to strong light, the positive will transmit or block the light in direct relationship to clear and opaque areas on the positive. The sensitized areas react chemically to this exposure and will wash away accordingly to form the stencil.

There are patented photo-stencil films that make the transfer method easier and faster than the direct method. What is more, not only is the stencilmaking procedure simple, but it is also easier to dissolve the stencil when you no longer need it. The direct method is a long procedure, yielding no better results for the effort involved, and it is almost an impossible task to dissolve the gelatin-coated screen of the direct photo stencil. We are here going to deal with the one best suited to the artist's needs, the transfer method.

MAKING THE TRANSPARENT POSITIVE

You may make the positive yourself or have a photoengraver do this for you from your sketch.

1. *Making your own positives. a.* Transparencies used. The positive may be made on any transparent or translucent material. This includes clear or frosted glass, clear or transparent acetate, fairly heavy tracing paper, patented tracing sheets such as Dull Mat or Trace-o-line, or even thin white bond paper that has been rubbed over with kerosene or oil. If the original sketch is done on thin white paper, it in itself may be used as a transparent positive, requiring no transfer or tracing.

b. Opaquing mediums used. The object of the opaquing medium is to make the positive opaque in the areas conforming to the black on the black-and-white original. Cut a piece of Trace-o-line tissue or other transparency large enough to cover the black-and-white drawing. Fasten it over the original with Scotch tape and paint in the design with the opaquing medium exactly as you see it through the transparency. Jet black India ink, black tempera or Japan paint, or professional photoengraver's opaquing medium may be used. One may also effectively employ black crayon or a soft-leaded pencil, especially when working on a rough-surfaced transparency such as frosted glass, etc. The slightly abrasive surface will be found sensitively receptive to crayon or pencil work and will produce a soft line comparable to Ross board or charcoal drawing.

2. *Photoengraver's positive.* If you are too busy or do not have the necessary materials, or if the drawing you want reproduced is so small and fine in detail that you couldn't possibly do justice to it by making your own positive in the actual size, then it might be well to call upon the services of a photoengraver.

For instance, if you wanted to reproduce an emblem with scrolls, extremely fine lettering, and other delicate work, you might prepare a black-and-white drawing on illustration board twice or three times the size that you want it ultimately reproduced. In other words, you work as large as you like. Then, when the black-and-white sketch is finished, you can send it to any photoengraver with the notation that you want it reduced and the image transferred to a transparent positive. This service doesn't cost much. The photoengraver's positive is used in the same way as a handmade positive.

The photoengraver can also make half-tone positives from regular photographs. For best results, no finer than an 85-line half-tone screen should be attempted with the photofilm available at present.

MATERIALS FOR MAKING THE STENCIL

1. *Transparent positive*. This is prepared in either of the ways previously described.

2. *Photo transfer film*. This is the film upon which the positive is exposed. It forms the substance of the stencil. Photo transfer film consists of a thin acetate or vinyl sheet supporting a layer of gelatin. It is available at silk screen supply dealers in sheets 20 by 30 inches. The film should be used within a few weeks after it is bought, as it deteriorates with time.

3. *Sensitizing solution*. This is the liquid with which the film is made sensitive to light. Some sensitizers come as ready-mixed liquids, but there are others that are sold in powder form and have to be compounded. Ask your dealer to give you the sensitizer meant for the film you are using. All sensitizing solutions deteriorate within a few weeks and should therefore be used before they spoil. The advantage in using the powder is that you mix only as much as you need at the time. The powder when not in solution can be kept for a long

time without the loss of chemical potency. It is best to store the ready-mixed solution in an amber bottle.

4. *Camel's-hair brush.* A soft 2-inch flexible brush is used to distribute the sensitizing fluid over the film. Use the best quality brush obtainable as there is nothing quite so annoying as a brush that sheds.

5. *Contact setup.* A contact frame is good for holding the positive in close contact with the sensitized film during exposure. In the absence of a professional contact frame, the following materials arranged in the same setup will serve very well and cost but little:

    a. Contact padding. A sponge, rubber, or felt pad large enough to hold the film and positive.

    b. Plate glass. Any heavy clear glass spotlessly clean, which is used to hold the positive in contact with the film.

6. *Lights.* A strong light passing through the positive will affect the sensitized film and bring about a chemical reaction. This may be provided by any intense source of light such as sunlight, a carbon arc lamp, or a photoflood bulb. A #2 photoflood bulb is recommended because it is inexpensive, has a life of about 6 exposure hours, and will fit any standard bulb socket. Sunlight, always difficult to control because its intensity fluctuates with the hour and the season, is not so reliable as artificial light, which can be regulated and controlled.

7. *Developing pan.* This is a shallow pan in which the film is bathed after it has been exposed. It may be made of

Fastening the film.

Sensitizing the film.

Drying the sensitized film.

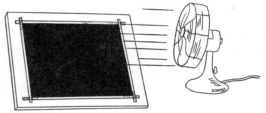

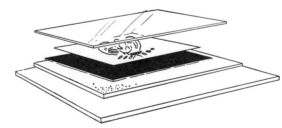

Making the contact setup.

Exposing the photofilm.

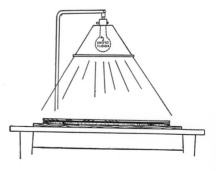

PLATE 21

porcelain, glass, or wood, but not of unprotected metal. The receptacle should be broad but shallow and large enough adequately to accommodate the film. If no pan is available, a stoppered enamel sink will do.

PROCEDURE FOR MAKING THE STENCIL (Refer to Plates 21, 22, and 23)

1. Cut the photofilm to size. The photofilm should be an inch or so larger all around than the design to be reproduced.

2. Fasten the film. Place the film, gelatin side up, on a sheet of glass or flat cardboard. Scotch-tape it well all around so that the film will lie perfectly flat.

3. Prepare the sensitizer. Use the sensitizer as directed on the label.

4. Sensitize the photofilm. Brush the sensitizing solution liberally over the film. To be sure that the entire film is covered, brush it several times, spreading it in a different direction each time. Work the sensitizer well into the film and be sure to get it on as smoothly as possible. Leave no puddles. Let the film dry in the dark on a flat table. While the sensitizer is wet, the film is not highly responsive to light. Sensitizing, therefore, does not require a special darkroom but can be done in subdued light.

5. Dry the sensitized film. The drying, as pointed out above, should take place in the dark. An electric fan will dry the film in about 15 minutes although it may take an hour or so to dry naturally. Be sure that the table on which the film reposes is free from dust, or as the film is fanned the dust will be agitated and will settle on the tacky surface.

6. Release the film. When the sensitized film is dry, the Scotch tape is removed, and the film released.

7. Prepare the contact setup. If you lack a professional contact frame, make use of the following arrangement, based on the contact frame principle: Place the contact padding on a sturdy table. Lay the film on top of this so that the sensitized gelatin side faces the mat. On top of this, place the positive so that the design is reversed and lettering appears as if seen in a mirror. Cover this with a clean sheet of heavy glass to keep the positive pressed firmly against the film.

8. Make the exposure setup. Rig up a photoflood bulb about 12 inches away from the contact setup and directly over it. The larger the positive, the further up the light should be, so that the rays of light may span the entire area.

9. Expose the stencil. Just as it is a matter of experienced guesswork to determine the strength of the acid in etching,

it is also a matter of calculated guessing to approximate the exposure time for a photo stencil. The length of exposure varies with the intensity of light, the degree of transparency of the positive, the type of work to be reproduced, the particular kind of photofilm used, the freshness of the sensitizer, etc. It is therefore impossible to set up an exposure time table that will apply under all conditions.

Each exposure time should be based on a series of trial exposures. From the results of these tests under known conditions, you can determine the best exposure schedule. Make these tests with the film, the sensitizer, and all other factors the same for the preliminary tests as for the actual exposure. In general, the following holds good:

a. The more intense the light, the less exposure time needed.

b. The more transparent the positive, the less exposure time needed. A clear glass positive will require less time than one on translucent paper.

c. The finer the detail, the less exposure time needed. Fine pen-and-ink line drawings or delicate halftones require less time than solid areas.

Manufacturers of some films make this recommendation (also subject to variations): using a #2 photoflood bulb 18 inches overhead, 2 minutes are required for clear positives of fine detail and 3 minutes for the same type of positive with broader design areas.

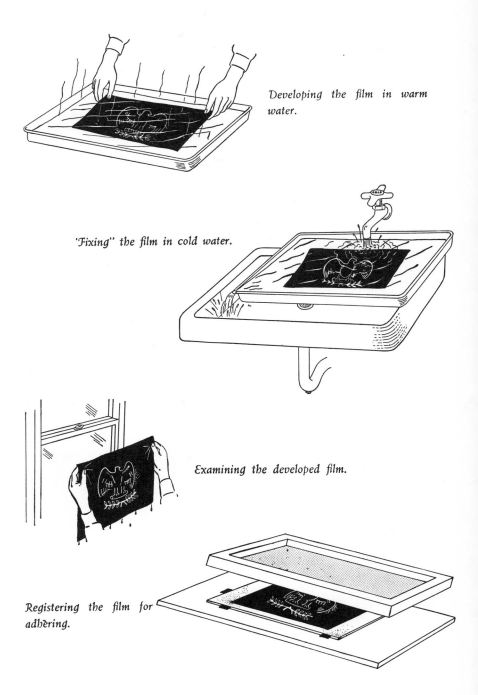

Developing the film in warm water.

"Fixing" the film in cold water.

Examining the developed film.

Registering the film for adhering.

114 PLATE 22

Each photofilm manufacturer will be glad to supply you with a set of instructions peculiar to his special type of film. An electric exposure meter will greatly facilitate the determination of the proper exposure time, as it is an infallible device for measuring light intensity.

10. Release the film. After the exposure is made, lift the contact glass and remove the film from the contact setup. The film has been affected in proportion to the light that has been transmitted through the positive.

11. Develop the film. Warm water will dissolve the part of the gelatin that was shielded from the light. This is done by immersing the film, gelatin side down, in a panful of moderately hot water (about 110 to 120° F.). Take it out after 5 minutes or so. Turn the film over and immerse it again with the gelatin side up. Agitate the water a little. The water will soon become discolored by the gelatin that is gradually washing away. Lift the film out of the water to check whether the desired parts are open. If the image has not completely washed out, place the film back in the bath and rub the fingers gently over the stubborn parts to wash them off or spray some water directly on the film. If the water bath cools or becomes very discolored, replace it with fresh warm water.

12. Fix the film. Bathe the film in a pan of cold water for a few minutes and let the water circulate so that a gentle cur-

Adhering the stencil.

Drying the stencil.

Stripping the backing sheet.

PLATE 23

rent flows over the film. This will cleanse the film, chill the gelatin, and arrest further development of the film, so that it will no longer be affected by light. The film is now ready to be transferred to the silk screen.

13. Adhere the film. To adhere the film to the silk, register the dripping wet film, gelatin side up, in the guides on the printing base. You may place a card in the guides first and lay the film over it. Be sure that the silk screen is perfectly clean and free from grease or dust. Lower the screen so that the underside of the silk is in perfect contact with the film.

Spread several layers of newspapers or blotters on the silk and use your hands or a rubber roller to make the newspapers absorb the moisture of the film as it penetrates the silk. As the newspapers become saturated with the water absorbed from the film underneath, put fresh dry paper sheets on the silk. Continue this blotting operation until no more moisture is in evidence. Remove all newspapers from the screen and fan the screen until it is dry.

14. Strip the photofilm. When the film is bone dry, it is safe to strip the backing sheet. Raise the screen and start at a corner of the celluloid backing sheet to peel it off the gelatin film. It should come off without any resistance. Keep in mind that the film must be perfectly dry before you strip it, or you may regret your impatience. If the backing sheet is lifted

Printed in one color from a photographic stencil. The original was done with crayon on Ross board, then photographed onto a transparent positive.

PLATE 24

while the film is still damp, it will pull some of the fine dots or lines of the gelatin with it, thus ruining a good stencil.

15. Mask out the silk. If the sheet of photofilm used was not large enough to cover the screen area, use lacquer, glue, or a paper mask to block out the open silk surrounding the photofilm, as in the NuFilm method. The stencil is now ready for printing.

The entire procedure for making a stencil photographically after the transparent positive has been prepared can be accomplished in less than two hours. A photo stencil will yield exceptionally sharp uniform prints with a variety of printing mediums such as oil process paints, colored lacquers, enamels, and others. Tempera colors can be used with success only for short runs. After a limited number of prints are run off, the water content of the tempera paint may attack the gelatin base of the film, thus dissolving the stencil. The paints used for the photo stencil should be extra fine and very "short." Photo screens are generally used for very fine line work or halftones, and unless the paint is of a creamy consistency, it will be impossible to get good results. Be sure that there is enough transparent base in the paint and that it is free from lumps and all foreign matter. The stencil may be stored after the paint has been removed and the screen cleaned for a future edition of the same print.

The beginner would do well to confine himself to one-color

Printed in one color from a photographic stencil. Miss Mary McQuaid, the artist, used opaquing ink to paint the drawing directly onto Trace-o-line. This transparent drawing served as the positive for the photographic stencil.

reproductions with the photo method. Good multicolor photographic work, employing the four-color process principle, is done commercially, but it is not within the province of the silk screen artist with limited studio equipment to enter that phase of the work.

DISSOLVING THE STENCIL

To dissolve a photo stencil like that which we have described, apply plenty of warm water to both sides of the screen. A pinch of powdered lye added to the water will help to dissolve any stubborn parts of the stencil which may resist the first water bath. Dry the screen and check to see that it is clean before you put it away.

No type of stencil other than the photographic could have produced work of so intricate a nature. One section of this repeat motif was made by hand, and a number of reduced photographic copies were pasted up to form an allover pattern. From this paste-up original, a photoengraver prepared the transparent positive needed to make the stencil.

PLATE 26

Scrap by Syd Fossum, 1954

Multicolor Printing

The Bay by Max A. Cohn

MULTICOLOR
PRINTING

THE various stencilmaking techniques described in preceding chapters have been intentionally confined to single-color work. The general principle and most of the procedure for making stencils for multicolor prints is the same as for one-color prints. This chapter will explain how stencils for two or more colors can be prepared to produce a perfectly registered print. Perfect register is vital to the success of your print.

If the color areas on the original are indistinct, work from a tracing where the color boundaries have been outlined. A separate stencil is required for each color, except where transparent colors are employed to overlap previous colors. An original, for instance, with red, black, and blue would require three stencils and three printings, one for each distinct color.

In any multicolor job, the first color is printed right through the entire lot. When this is dry, the second color is applied, and so on. Usually, especially in longer editions, there is no waiting for drying, because by the time the last prints of the

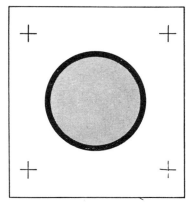

Original drawing to be reproduced.

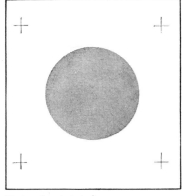

First color printed.

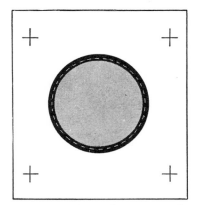

Relation of first color to second, showing overdraw.

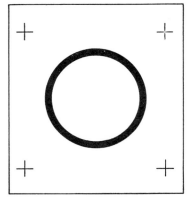

Second color made exact size.

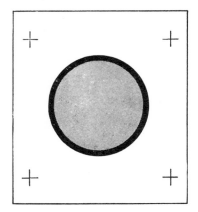

Coinciding crossmarks, indicating good register.

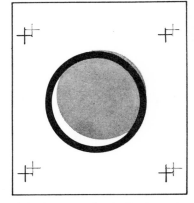

Shifted crossmarks, indicating mis-register.

Use of crossmarks as a guide to registration.

PLATE 27

first color are made, the first prints are dry, and you can go ahead with the next color.

Although each color requires an individual *stencil*, one *screen* may be used for all the colors of a multicolor job. When one color is run off, the stencil may be dissolved and the same screen unit used for the next color. Of course, most stencils can be stored for future reruns. If you want to save the stencils, you will have to have as many screens as colors in the job, and each screen will have to fit the master printing base, with the same register guides used for all the colors. There are occasions when one *stencil* can be used to print two or more distinct colors on the same job. Here is an example of a practical application of this multicolor, single-stencil idea. If two colors on a painting are separated from each other, only one stencil is made for printing both colors at the same time. The screen is then partitioned into two compartments with a piece of cardboard. The colors are poured into their respective compartments, and, with the aid of small squeegees, both colors are printed simultaneously. These colors may be printed together as just described, or they may be printed individually, one color at a time, by printing one color while stopping out the other area on the stencil with a sheet of paper under the silk. Regardless of the number of stencils used, a painting can be reproduced in any number of colors and registered with hairline accuracy.

The key to multicolor registration lies in the *register-guide* system, whereby you can accurately synchronize any number of colors to form a perfectly registered facsimile of your original. The register guides, fastened to the printing bed as shown in Plate 5, make registration a mechanically accurate routine, removing all guesswork in the placement of the card to be printed. The same guides are used for all the colors on a painting. To test the efficacy of the guides, try this: Place a card into the register guides and pull a paint impression. Reregister the card and take another proof. If the card has been placed into the guides accurately both times, the paint should print in exactly the same position. Theoretically a print can be reregistered in this manner any number of times with the same results.

Let us start with an elementary problem in registration. Let us assume that we are to reproduce a design in two distinct colors, a narrow black band surrounding a solid red circle. The first thing to decide is the order in which the colors are to be printed. There are no steadfast rules for determining the sequence of colors. Each drawing has to be carefully analyzed to see which sequence to favor. In most cases, use the same judgment as you do in painting by hand. If, for instance, a drawing calls for a vast blue sky spotted with a few black birds in flight, print the entire sky first and then superimpose the birds. The order of colors should be listed somewhere in the margin of the drawing. This marginal note will be especially helpful when so many colors are planned that it would be difficult to remember the sequence.

In order to have a constant check on the accuracy of the register in multicolor work, the following system, universally employed by lithographers and print makers, is used in screen printing:

Draw a fine cross in each of the four corners of the margin of the original, as seen in Plate 27. These thin 1/2 inch lines crossing each other at right angles may be drawn in pencil or ink.

The crossmarks are duplicated on the stencil for each color, as if they were part of the design. For each color, therefore, the crossmarks will show as part of the print. In the perfectly registered job, the marks for the last in a series of colors will coincide exactly with all the previous crossmarks. If the margin is to be trimmed off after the printing, the crossmarks should appear on every print. If no margin is allowed, or if the margin is to remain as part of the picture, these marks appear only on several master prints. They are then stopped out on the stencil, and the entire edition is printed without them. For the next color, the same master cards are again printed, the register checked, and the crossmarks on the stencil stopped out as before. The same master register sheets are used for all subsequent colors. In our illustrated job, because of the simplicity of the color areas, it would be easy enough to see that the print is out of register without referring to crossmarks. Where the relation between colors in a print is not so discernible until all the colors have been printed, it may not be so easy to detect misregister without the crossmarks.

Rockport by Leonard Pytlak.   *Size of print 13½ by 19 inches.*
Fifteen stencils were used to produce this print, but a study of the actual print will reveal twenty-two distinct colors. This disparity between the number of stencils and the number of resulting colors is the result of print-

If the crossmarks of one color do not register with those of previous colors, the entire print is out of register. The amount by which the crossmarks fail to coincide indicates the extent of misregister. If the four crossmarks for one color all appear off in the same way, then the registration may be corrected by shifting the register guides on the printing base to fit the crosses.

Although the guide system offers a dependable means of registration, other factors that affect registration must be taken into cognizance when the stencils for a multicolor job are made. Faulty registration may be caused by an indiscernible "give" in the silk or in the printing frame, a loosening up of the screws in the hinges, loose guides, or pure carelessness in setting the cards into the guides. Whatever the cause, some means obviously must be provided to allow for a margin of error—human or mechanical. Overdrawing one color into another will provide the margin of safety.

When making the stencil for the red, overdraw the circle 1/16 inch all around so that the red will print that much larger than it appears on the original sketch. The extension of the first color into the second will compensate for any possible discrepancies in register during printing. The stencil for the black outline does not require any overdraw, as it is the final color to be printed. In jobs involving more than two colors, make similar allowances to assure good register.

If opaque colors are used on the job we are describing, the

Noah's Dory by Elizabeth Olds.

This is printed in a number of colors, with more than one color appearing on the same stencil. While one color was being printed, the others were blocked out with a paper mask. The actual print radiates with rich color, well distributed in the composition.

Size of print 13 by 24 inches.

PLATE 29

black band will completely obliterate the overdrawn extension of the red circle. If transparent colors are used, the transparent black printed over the red will show a blackish brown
rim between the black band and the red circle. In other
words, this can become a three-color job with only two printings. It may be seen that by overlapping colors in the proper
sequence, the extension of one transparent color over another
transparent or opaque color will yield additional colors and
shades. Where such additional tones are not desirable, however, no overdraw should be made. This, of course, will call
for extra care in the registration of transparent color prints.
The possibilities of transparencies will be further explored in
the chapter on colors.

BLENDING

Although the silk screen process is much better equipped to
reproduce flat color effects, a certain amount of blending or
shading can be accomplished if the blend is gradual and fol-
lows in a straight line. This means that although it would be
impossible to blend a circle of concentric shades, an open
background such as a sky where the color changed from a
golden orange at the horizon to a bluish pink above could be
managed nicely. See Plates 30 and 31.

As it is the paint, not the stencil, that determines the blend,
prepare your stencils the same way as for solid-tone printing.
Use individual containers for mixing the colors that you re-

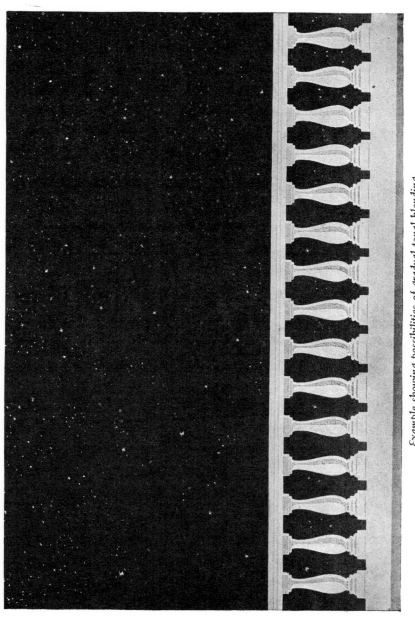

Example showing possibilities of gradual tonal blending.

PLATE 30

quire. For the sky we mentioned, you might mix three colors, orange, yellow, and pale blue. Be sure that all the colors are of the same consistency. Pour the orange, yellow, and blue paints into their proper relative positions on the screen, corresponding to their appearance on the sky. Use a squeegee that is large enough to take in all three colors at one time, and squeegee as you would when printing solid colors. Don't be disappointed if the blending doesn't take place magically at once. The first few prints will show horizontal bands of distinct colors. Run several proof sheets until these lines of demarcation diminish and the shades merge. You will soon see a smooth transition of tone, which means that you may begin to print on your good stock. You will find that no two prints are exactly alike, because as the squeegeeing continues, and the colors run into one another more and more, they gradually lose their identities. After you have made about a dozen good prints, replenish the colors in your screen in the original relationship and continue as before.

As may be seen, this is a slow process, but the results usually prove commensurate with the effort.

The Cove by Hicken

CHAPTER TEN

Color

The Animal by Mach, 1950

National Serigraph Society

Surf by Harry Shokler

COLOR

The silk screen process is the only printing process which can be employed to print on any flat surface with a practically unlimited choice of printing mediums. This versatility is clarified by a review of the silk screen principle. Here is a stencil with openings that are impartial to any viscous fluid. Tempera color, oil color, dyes, and lacquers can pass through the stencil with equal facility. But these are not just ordinary paints or dyes; they are especially prepared for use with the process; they must be of the proper consistency and flexibility, and they must have a controlled drying property.

Fortunately, because of the industrial demand for these printing mediums, the fine artist can share with the commercial process printers paints and inks that have been developed through scientific experimentation. In the preparation of these printing mediums, paint chemists have combined the paints with the proper varnishes and vehicles, driers and oils, and all the rest that is necessary to make each medium especially suited to silk screen work.

The most widely used printing medium is process oil color.

Tempera water colors, however, are fast finding new adherents among fine print makers. Lacquers, dyes, and special textile paints are successfully used for screening on cloth. It is recommended, however, that the silk screen novitiate control his experimental impulses and, for a while at least, confine himself to oil colors.

PROCESS OIL COLORS

Oil colors, or process oil colors as they are called to differentiate them from regular palette colors, offer the greatest range of effects of any type of paint used for process work. They are by nature waterproof and opaque, with excellent covering qualities. They make it possible to print a light color over a dark one; a white will not lose its opacity even on a dark ground. Oil colors can be combined with many types of varnishes to produce different desirable results. Ordinarily, oil colors dry flat, with a dull mat finish. If for any reason a shiny finish is preferred, gloss varnish may be added to the paint. Where a transparent effect seems suitable, opaque oil colors can be reduced to any degree of transparency by the addition of a compound known as *transparent base*. Process oil paints may be used with any type of stencil. They will work equally well with the photographic, paper, glue, and film stencils. There is nothing in this paint to attack the stopping-out medium of any stencil.

These are among the factors that endow oil colors with a

virtuosity not shared by other silk screen printing mediums and that help to equip the artist to meet almost any printing requirement.

Process oil paints are put up in pints, quarts, gallons, and even five- and ten-gallon drums. As artists, your purchases will undoubtedly be limited to pints and quarts. The authors as artists have found the paints and varnishes of the following manufacturers consistently satisfactory: Devoe and Raynolds of Chicago; Naz-Dar of Chicago; T. J. Ronan of New York, the Serascreen Corp. of New York, and Union Ink of East Rutherford, N. J. Addresses of other silk screen manufacturers may be had by consulting the classified phone directory of your city. The *Signs of the Times*, a national journal (Cincinnati, Ohio) devoted to the industrial use of silk screen, will also be a helpful reference source of dealers.

Process oil paints cannot be used just as they come from the can. Generally they are too heavy to be used without first being thinned. They should be thinned with varnish, but in an emergency kerosene or turpentine may be substituted. If turpentine is used to excess, the color will dry so fast that it will clog the mesh of the silk. Too much kerosene will have the opposite effect; it will retard the drying of the paint.

To make any color transparent, a clear transparent base is mixed with the paint, the quantity of base added determining the degree of transparency. In buying a transparent base, bear in mind that there are two kinds: a clear base, which looks

Houses Near the B and A by Edward Landon. *Size of print 14 by 20 inches.* The white paper showing through in many places reflects a spontaneity characteristic of an original water color. Ten colors, some opaque and others transparent, were used in stenciling this print.

PLATE 32

and feels like vaseline, and a cheaper base, which resembles putty. A clear base will not rob colors of their true brilliance regardless of the quantity added, whereas the cheaper base will upset the color value of the paint with which it is mixed. The cheaper grade is commonly used in commercial work as an economy measure in order to extend the paint and make larger coverage possible.

As transparent color will naturally reveal any colors that it overlaps, it makes many effects possible. By printing a transparent blue over a yellow, for example, you may obtain a free third color, green. Or you may add enough base to the paint to reduce it to a pure tint, which will produce the tonal quality of an original water color. Paints can be made sufficiently thin and transparent to make the texture of the paper part of the picture, adding a freshness and luminosity to the print. Transparent base may be used in conjunction with varnish, if you bear in mind that the varnish will affect the finish of the print.

PROCESS TEMPERA COLORS

This is a comparatively new medium and is becoming increasingly popular for noncommercial uses. It is odorless and noninflammable. The paint may be thinned and the screen cleaned with plain water, thus doing away with the expense of varnishes and special solvents. Paint spots on hands and clothing are easily removed. Tempera colors are unusually brilliant and fresh looking, and this fact, combined with their natural transparency, makes for a fluid translucency not easily attainable with other mediums. Another good point about tempera colors is that they dry within 5 to 15 minutes, making it possible to print colors in rapid succession without losing time. Tempera colors do have several shortcomings, which may be overcome by paint chemists in the future. For one thing, they cannot be used successfully with organdy screens. The water in the paint destroys the natural sizing of the organdy, making it limp and soggy. Tempera colors printed on thin paper will warp and wrinkle the paper as the paint dries. Tempera water colors are naturally transparent; therefore you cannot print a light color on a darker surface. The only opaque tempera colors are white and black. All other colors, and there is quite an array of them, are transparent. Although the colors are transparent, they can be made even more so with special transparent base. Be sure not to use the oil color transparent base as that would be a mistake you would never forget—it is virtually like trying to mix oil and water. This paint also has a tendency to cling to the blade of the squeegee, making it necessary to shake the squeegee from time to time to remove the accumulated paint.

Tempera colors are limited to stencils where glue is not a stopping-out medium. This immediately eliminates the tusche-glue stencil and the glue-block-out stencil. The reason for this is apparent. Since the tempera color contains water, it would not take long for the paint to dissolve the glue and ruin the stencil.

It must be pointed out that tempera water colors are not necessarily the only type of colors used for simulating water-color paintings. A wash effect is also obtainable with oil colors to which transparent base has been added. Ordinary tempera colors, or show-card colors, cannot be used for silk screen work. They dry into the mesh of the silk, and after several impressions the silk becomes clogged. The Artone Company of New York and the Devoe and Raynolds Company of Chicago produce tempera colors specifically prepared for silk screen stenciling.

MISCELLANEOUS MEDIUMS

Industrial demands for printing mediums off the beaten path have led to the development of such diverse mediums as lacquers, enamels, dyes, glass-etching compounds, etc. These are somewhat beyond the scope of the print maker, rather troublesome to beginners, and are generally reserved for commercial printing jobs. Henceforth, all instructions pertaining to paints will apply to oil process colors except where otherwise stated.

THE PALETTE

Silk screen printing paints are available in many colors. You can get an idea of the full range from any dealer's catalogue. It's hardly necessary, though, for an artist with a practical background in color theory to purchase every color in the catalogue. It is indeed a rare occurrence when standard colors are used right out of the can without undergoing some intermixing with other colors in order to be lightened, subdued, or changed in some other way to get just the right match.

This color sensitivity is one of the factors distinguishing the fine-art print from the commercial print. Commercial silk screen work is often characterized by a harshness of color due to the printer's following the course of least resistance. In the rush of things, a standard color closest in range to the one to be matched is often poured into the screen without intermixing. An artist, on the other hand, is meticulous about the exactness of color value. As he becomes adept at intermixing process colors, he will be able to obtain every nuance of shade that he desires in his print.

In the main, the following palette of oil colors and varnishes is suggested. The arbitrary quantities stated should be enough to get an artist started. With this palette it is possible to mix and match any color in the spectrum.

> One pint of mineral orange
> One pint of vermillion red
> One pint of magenta
> One pint of lemon yellow
> One pint of chrome yellow
> One pint of turquoise blue

One pint of ultramarine blue
One quart of white
One quart of black
One quart of quick-drying reducing varnish
One pint of slow-drying flexible varnish
One pint of overprint varnish
One gallon of clear transparent base

VARNISHES

The kind of varnish put into the paint determines the drying time, the finish, and the flexibility of the print. Paint combined with slow-drying varnish may require from 4 to 6 hours
for thorough drying. The varnish acts as a flexible binder, especially important when printing on nonabsorbent surfaces.
If reducing varnish is used, the paint may dry in an hour or
even less. Drying time depends not only on the varnish, but
also on the weather, the thickness of the layer of paint, and
the surface upon which it is applied. It will take longer for
paint to dry on glass than on absorbent paper. Paint applied
partly over raw stock and partly over a previously printed
color will dry faster on the paper than over the other coat
of paint.

As varnish is considerably less viscous than the paint to
which it is added, the more varnish that is added, the thinner
the paint becomes. Reducing varnish added to the paint will
not impede the drying quality of the paint. For a high gloss,

or where the paint has to be extra flexible for printing on celluloid, cloth, or any material to be bent, folded, or draped, there is a gloss varnish—gummy, flexible, and slow-drying. There is also an overprint varnish for inducing a gloss on limited areas or over the entire face of the print. This is not mixed in with the paint; it is applied through a stencil over the basic color work.

In most cases, the paints and varnishes of one manufacturer will be compatible with those of another and can be intermixed. Occasionally you run across synthetic products that cannot be mixed with others. It is best, therefore, to buy the complete assortment from one reliable dealer. Then you know that the paints and varnishes you have are made for each other.

MATCHING AND MIXING COLORS

Anyone experienced in matching colors knows that natural daylight is best for such work. Artificial light is deceiving, as it distorts color values. If your interest in this new graphic art carries you into working into the night, provide yourself with a fluorescent tube light or at least a blue daylight bulb, both of which come close to approximating daylight.

A good rule to remember in matching colors is that it is always easier to darken a color than to make it lighter. When mixing a gray with white and black, it is better to start with the white and add black slowly until you have the desired shade of gray. Paint should be completely mixed before it is poured into the screen. If you find it too heavy for printing, do not try to thin the color by pouring varnish into the screen. Do it the right way. Scoop up the paint, pour it back into the can, add the necessary varnish, and stir thoroughly. Try the paint again. If you do it this way, you are sure that the paint and the varnish are completely integrated and that the entire quantity of paint for this job will be of uniform working consistency.

MIXING COLORS FOR OPAQUE PRINTING

Let us assume that you want to match a maroon, a color which does not appear on the palette on page 146. The color components of this shade of maroon may include magenta, vermillion, ultramarine blue, black, chrome yellow, well nigh all the colors at our disposal. We take a finger dab of these colors and rub them together on a piece of white cardboard. It may be found necessary to take a little more magenta, or even a touch of white, to produce the particular shade of maroon we are after. This conglomerate mixture gives us an idea of the relative proportions of the various colors that go to make up the color we want. When we are satisfied that the resulting color swatch approximates the color on the original that we want to match, we can mix the paint in bulk, using these same proportions.

Get a can or other container and check to see that it is

clean. The can should be large enough to accommodate more paint than you expect to mix. This is to allow for the subsequent addition of varnish needed to thin the color. Place a quantity of each of the colors in the estimated proportions into your mixing can. Use a separate spoon or stick for scooping out each color. Blend the component colors in the mixing can until the color is matched; then add varnish for the right consistency. Stir the entire contents thoroughly to be sure that the varnish and the colors are completely intermixed, as insufficient stirring will cause streaks of unmixed color in the print.

The question might arise as to how much paint to mix and just how thin or thick it should be. Paint manufacturers tell us that one gallon of paint will cover from 750 to 1000 square feet of printing area. This may not be enlightening to the artist unconcerned with hundreds of square feet. To reduce these industrial statistics to the artist's limited printing needs, let us refer to the frontispiece of this book. A pint of prepared color, properly thinned, would be more than enough for 3,000 maroon impressions. The amount of coverage will naturally vary with the surface upon which the color is applied. Highly absorbent stock will drink in the varnish of the paint, thus reducing the coverage. A nonabsorbent surface will extend the coverage to perhaps more than the 800 square feet per gallon.

As to consistency, that too varies with the surface upon

which the printing is to be done. Thinner paint should be used on soft, absorbent surfaces, such as paper and cloth, than on metal or glass. Paint that is too thin or loose will smudge on nonabsorbent surfaces. Paint for printing on paper should be of the consistency of molasses, or, forsaking this analogy and resorting to a practical test, let us see how you can gauge the consistency of your paint mixture. After you have mixed the paint and stirred it well, raise the mixing spoon. If it is the proper consistency for printing on paper, the paint should drop rather than run down the spoon. The paint should roll rather than flow when the can is tipped, and you should feel a slight resistance to the spoon as you mix the paint.

Paint that has been mixed and matched as described should now be tested through a screen to make a final comparison with the color we are trying to match. Rubbing the color on with the fingers cannot be depended upon, as the colors may turn out to be quite different when screened through the silk. For this reason, it is good practice to use a small trial screen with inside dimensions about 6 by 10 inches, to be exclusively reserved for testing paints. This little screen should be hinged to a base of appropriate size and should have a small squeegee as part of the testing apparatus. A little paint is put into the screen and squeegeed over a card of the same color and texture as that to be used on the regular run. The screened swatch of color is then put aside and allowed to dry. The paint is removed from the test screen, and the screen is washed. You are not ready to go ahead with the printing itself until the color sample proof is dry and "o.k.'d."

When the swatch has dried, you may be surprised to discover that the shade has changed slightly. On the basis of this observation, it may be necessary to remix the paint, altering the proportions slightly, and then to make other tests, until the printed color swatch dries in the exact shade desired. A test screen should be made part of the equipment of every printer who is concerned with the close matching of colors. It is less troublesome to clean the small screen than a large one.

If you have inadvertently made the paint too soupy by the addition of an excessive amount of varnish, you may correct your indiscretion by adding transparent base to the thin color. Stir the base well into the paint mixture. Transparent base is made for such an exigency. The gelatinous substance of which the base is composed has the property of jelling the color, making it thicker and "shorter." A short paint is one that does not flow or run too easily. There is, however, a danger of putting in too much shortener. Transparent base also causes colors to become transparent in direct proportion to the amount of base added. That is not serious with black paint, as black will retain its characteristic opacity in spite of a quantity of base. If too much base is added to red, blue, or other colors, however, they will become so transparent as to lose the covering quality necessary to retain certain color values.

MIXING COLORS FOR TRANSPARENT PRINTING

The technical problems and possibilities of transparencies are manifold. Matching and mixing colors for the printing of transparent paints entails considerable experience and many test proofs. It is a rather tricky job because the transparent color appears different on the paper than it does in the can. What looks like an intense blue in the can may turn out an insipid pale blue when screened. A transparent color overlapped on other colors will appear as a different shade and sometimes an entirely different color. In printing transparent colors, you will need a separate stencil for every fundamental color, but secondary colors will result from printing one color over another, such as green from blue and yellow, orange from yellow and red, purple from red and blue, etc. As many as three, four, and even more transparent colors may be printed one on top of the other to produce shades and tones not actually mixed in the paint pot. To predetermine what superimposition is necessary requires a fundamental knowledge of color, as well as experience based on trial and error. Experimentation with different stencils, effects, and color combinations may sometimes lead to such unusual results that even experts will be baffled in trying to figure out how a certain effect was obtained.

Let us see what steps to take to get the transparent paint to look like the one we are trying to match. Match up a small quantity of opaque process paint to the desired shade. If you need a quart of transparent color, start with a tablespoonful of matched opaque paint. Put half a quart of transparent base into a clean can capable of holding more than a quart. Add varnish for the proper consistency and stir well. Uneven mixture of transparent base with the color may give you pock-marked tones in the print. Add half a spoonful of your matched opaque color to the thinned base and mix this well. You will find that even so little color has tinted the entire transparent base mixture. Make several test prints with your small screen, using samples of the stock upon which the regular edition is to be printed. Allow the color swatches to dry and compare them to the color you want. Do not be dismayed if the first tests are not successful; it would be just a lucky chance if they were. If the tests show that the color is too pale, it may be necessary to add a few more drops of the opaque color, or even a little opaque color not part of the original spoonful. If the tests show that the color is too dark, you may add a touch of white or a little more transparent base.

The type of squeegee used is especially important when printing with transparent colors. The same color may screen much deeper and more intense with a soft-rubber than with a hard-bladed squeegee. Or for that matter, the same squeegee can produce different shades if the pressure exerted on it is altered during printing. For instance, a light scrape allows a thicker deposit of paint, and makes the color more intense. A heavy scrape makes the transparent color appear lighter on the finished print. The paper also plays a part. The grain and finish of the stock will affect the particular texture and color of the paint.

When you do a multicolor job involving transparent colors, save at least one of each of the progressive proofs that went into making the complete print. These will serve as an excellent index of the tones that were achieved by overlapping certain colors. Perhaps not all the colors in the finished print will meet with your approval, but you will have learned from the results of this contact with printing transparencies how to avoid the same pitfalls in future work.

These progressive proofs serve another purpose. You may have a limited number of screens in your studio and be unable to file any for future reprints. Under such circumstances, you may wash out your screens as necessary, making them available for new designs. Your progressive proofs will serve as color separations to guide you in remaking the stencils and matching each color accordingly.

TONERS

In printing transparent colors, you may use either regular opaque process paint to tint the transparent base or what are commonly known as *toners*. These are specially concentrated pigment colors of the consistency of heavy printer's ink. Toners are available in many colors and, like process paints, may be intermixed to produce shades not available in ready-mixed form. Toners are preferable to process colors because a little goes a long way and because they introduce a purity of tone in highly transparent color. Artist's tube oil colors or regular printer's inks mix well with transparent base and can also be used as toners.

FLUORESCENT COLORS

These are super brilliant paints which give off a luminosity far exceeding that of any standard paints. These paints are especially formulated for screen process work and come in a limited palette of colors. They can be screened in much the same way as standard colors, but are much more costly and should therefore be used with restraint. It is generally better to confine the use of these brilliant paints to limited areas in order to avoid gaudiness, which is never in good taste, but that is a personal matter for each artist, and hardly the subject of this chapter.

Let us assume that you want to make a pint of gold paint. Pour a few tablespoonfuls of special bronzing liquid into a clean container. (Heavy, slow-drying varnish has the same binding property as this liquid and may be substituted for it.) Add a spoonful of the gold powder and stir thoroughly. Add some more bronzing liquid and again some powder. Continue to alternate these ingredients and to stir well, until you have mixed the needed amount.

To allow the powder in suspension to pass through the

mesh of the silk, metallic pastes should be mixed to a thinner consistency than ordinary paint. If the heavy varnish has made the paint too gummy, add a few drops of turpentine. This will cut the paint and take away some of the tackiness.

Mix only as much paint as you require at the time, because any leftover paint will tarnish and lose its brilliance, even if it stands only overnight. Stir the mixture well each time before pouring it into the screen, as the metallic powder has a tendency to settle in the bronzing liquid or varnish with which it was mixed.

In spite of the bother that it may appear to be, buying the powder and mixing it yourself assures you a brilliancy that the ready-mixed metallic paints cannot match.

CARE OF PAINTS

When not in use, all paints should be well covered. If left open for a considerable length of time, oxidation will produce a hard crust on the paint. The volatile oils will slowly dry out, leaving the paint lumpy. If this has happened to your colors, they can still be redeemed, but they will have to be strained first. This, in the main, is the procedure for straining:

With a stick, palette knife, or spoon, remove the crust that has formed on top; then add some varnish to bring the paint back to a free-flowing consistency. Stir to mix the paint well with the varnish. The actual straining may be done with cheesecloth, gauze, or a fine-meshed wire strainer or sieve.

Place the cheesecloth over the mouth of a clean container, pushing it into the can slightly to form a pocket for the paint. Fasten the straining cloth to the can with a string or rubber band.

Pour paint into the strainer, almost filling the pocket. The weight of the paint will help to push it through the mesh. If you are in a hurry or just can't stand idly by, you can hasten the straining by agitating the paint with a spoon or stick. A residue of hard, undiluted lumps of paint may remain unstrained. These should be removed from the strainer before the next quantity of paint is poured in. Refill the strainer until all the paint is strained.

If a sieve is used, get one that is smaller than the mouth of the can, so that its pocket may extend into the can and the paint may go in without spilling. When the straining is finished, the sieve must be cleaned of all paint. A kerosene-soaked rag wiped over the mesh will remove any plugged-in particles of paint and make the strainer serviceable again.

If through the use of transparent base, paint has been made so heavy that it will not pass through cheesecloth or a sieve, there is another procedure for straining it. Soap your hands well and allow the lather to dry into your skin to form an invisible glove. Place a piece of cheesecloth over the opening of a clean container, pushing it inward to form a pocket. Pour some paint into this pocket, holding the cheesecloth with one hand to keep it from falling in. Quickly bring the ends of the cheesecloth together to form a closed bag for the paint. Holding this bag over the can with one hand, use the other hand to squeeze the bag with a downward and inward pressure. By milking downward from the neck, you will cause the paint to flow into the can rather than to the side of it. Continue this until the bag is empty, except for the unstrainable residue. Place the bag over a piece of old cardboard and remove the lumps that resisted straining by scraping the cloth with a palette knife or spoon. Use the same cloth again in the same way until all the paint is strained. Paint thus strained will have a creamy texture and will be as good as new. Naturally, the thinner the paint, the faster it will strain. But don't let this tempt you to thin the color without regard to its required printing consistency. To remove the paint from your hands, wipe them with a kerosene-soaked rag. Use a dry cloth to remove diluted paint. Wash your hands with soap and warm water to get the smell of kerosene off and to remove any remaining stains.

Old paint, as we have seen, can be redeemed, but not without going through this trouble. Even reading about this mild ordeal may dramatize to you the importance of keeping paint cans closed tightly when not in use. A special effort should also be made to keep cans clean and free from paint accumulations around the rim.

As a special precaution against air seeping into a can once opened, pour some slow-drying varnish or bronzing liquid to cover the top surface of the paint and close the can as tightly as possible. Paints so protected may be stored for months, without fear of having them dry up. If the cover should not be completely tight, the layer of varnish may harden into a thin flexible disk, but the paint itself will remain the same. When needed again, the loose varnish, or the hardened disk, is carefully removed, and the paint is found unimpaired.

New paints are now available which do not dry up in the can and therefore do not require these leak proof precautions. These paints are smooth to work with, dry within 15 or 20 minutes, and can be left in the screen for hours without drying into the mesh and clogging the silk. One of these lines goes under the trade name of P.D.Q. and is sold by the Serascreen Corp. of New York. Other brands are available at various dealers throughout the country.

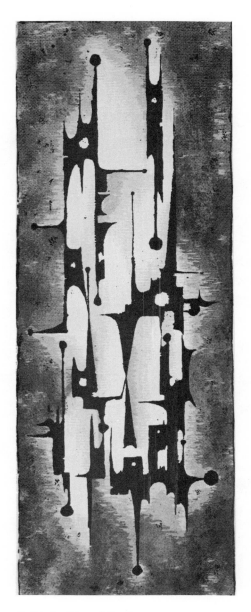

Gothic by Edward Landon, 1954
Metropolitan Museum of Art

CHAPTER ELEVEN

Circus Horses by Rose

PRINTING

HERE is too much artistic judgment and discrimination involved in making a fine silk screen print to delegate this important job to a professional printer. It is a rare commercial printer who possesses the combination of artistry and technical skill demanded for fine print making. The work of stencilmaking, color matching, and printing are inseparable techniques, and all play an important part in the artistic results of the print. Fine silk screen reproduction is not a mechanical process. It stands between printing and easel painting and requires an artist's sensitive care as well as more experimental time than the average commercial printer can afford.

It is different in commercial silk screen work, where a definite number of opaque colors are employed. If the colors are indicated properly, any reputable process establishment can match up the colors and run the job. It may be said that a commercial poster is a literal translation of the artist's sketch, while a fine-art print is an interpretative or free translation of an artist's conception. The subtle blendings, the free use of transparencies, and the infinite number of effects can be rendered sympathetically only by a true artist, preferably the one whose artistic creation is involved.

Setup for printing.

PLATE 33

As silk screen printing, or silk screen painting as we might call it, is not an expensive process as far as equipment goes, limited editions of prints can easily be taken care of in the average studio. Assuming that your stencils are ready and the paints matched and mixed, we now follow the step-by-step procedure of the printing operation.

The first thing that we must do is check on the make-ready. Are the hinges screwed down tight? Are the guides fastened firmly? Is the squeegee well sharpened? These are some of the questions which have to be answered affirmatively before it is safe to go ahead. The pushpins in the hinges must be pushed in all the way in order to interlock the hinge mates. If there is a little play in the hinges due to a worn pin, remove the pin, bend it slightly with a hammer, and force it back into the hinges.

And now let us look at our squeegee. There are two kinds of squeegees that can be used. The one-hand squeegee has a grip handle attached to the center. This squeegee is manipulated with one hand while the free hand rests on the printing frame. The other type of squeegee is the two-hand squeegee. This one has no handle; the case itself is used as the grip. The style of squeegee doesn't affect the print in any way; it's purely a matter of personal preference.

The squeegee should be at least 1 inch larger than the width of the design to be printed. If the squeegee is too small, two scrapes will have to be used to cover the area, and a streak mark will show where the two scrapes overlap. Before printing, always examine the rubber blade to see whether it requires attention. If it does, scrape it back and forth a few times in long, even strokes on a special sandpaper board. When sharpening it, be sure to hold the squeegee so that the entire bottom edge of the rubber receives the benefit of contact with the abrasive surface. About a dozen strokes should be enough to sharpen a blade that has become slightly dulled. See that there are no nicks or cuts in the rubber, or your prints will show streaks where the nicks don't carry the paint along.

If a nick is too deep to be fixed by sandpapering, trim off a slice of rubber the whole length of the blade to give the squeegee a new printing edge. It will require more than one cut to go through the rubber. To make sure that the edge comes out smooth and even, use a sharp mat knife with a long metal ruler as a guide. Sandpaper the edge well. Trimming the squeegee rubber should be turned to as a last resort because it is a difficult job and because in shortening the blade, you make it less flexible to the pressure of printing.

With the guides checked and the squeegee just right, get the paint and printing stock ready. The stock should be as large as the original card, because your register guides were set up according to the size of the original. Raise the screen and place one of the cards on the base, sliding it into the guides. First see that the card is flush against the two bottom guides and then slide it over until it is also set against the side guide. Keep your eyes on what you are doing and feel the card contacting the three guides. Lower the screen. Pour some paint into the screen along one of the banks, close to the frame. There is no measured quantity of paint poured in at one time, as the amount of paint that can be put into the screen will depend on how large the screen is and how much printing area there is. The stencil will admit only a thin layer of paint regardless of how large a reserve of paint there may be in the screen. Don't, however, put so much paint in that it will overflow when the screen is raised.

If this is your first attempt at silk screen printing, start with just a few spoonfuls of paint and see how many impressions you get from that amount. If you can control more paint without spilling or splashing, pour in a greater quantity the next time you refill the screen. In a stencil with large areas, you will naturally use up more paint for each impression than on a stencil with small openings. You will soon learn the right amount of paint to use.

And now for the actual printing. With the paint to one side of the screen, say on the right bank, place the squeegee on the screen and rub it up and down slightly. This will distribute the paint so that there is a ribbon of paint in front of the entire length of the rubber blade. Holding it firmly, pass the squeegee across the screen from right to left. Lift the screen and gaze upon your first print impression.

Just a few words about the technique of operating the squeegee. If you are using a one-hand squeegee, grip the handle with your right hand, rest your left hand on the printing frame, and push the squeegee from right to left, for one impression. For the next impression, reverse the procedure. Grip the squeegee handle with the left hand and, resting your right hand on the frame, push the squeegee back from left to right. This changing from side to side and from hand to hand is repeated throughout the printing.

If you are using a two-hand squeegee, when the squeegee is at rest on the right bank, this is what you do. Hold the farther end of the squeegee with the left hand and the nearer end with the right hand. Thus, holding the squeegee with both hands, pass it across the screen from right to left. For the next print reverse the procedure. The right hand goes to the farther end, the left hand to the nearer end, and the squeegee is passed from left to right. Regardless of the kind of squeegee used, be as sensitive to it as you would be to any intimate tool. Exert an evenly distributed downward pressure throughout the length of the squeegee. Sluggish or unbalanced pressure will distribute an uneven coat of paint. Feel the rubber blade do its part. Feel it push the paint through the screen. Feel the smooth contact with the silk. If you find that you leave a pool of paint in the wake of your squeegee, you know that the squeegee is not performing its true function, that of forcing an even, clean coat of paint through to the printing stock. If everything else is under control, a good even sweep of the squeegee should leave the silk free from paint.

While you manipulate the squeegee, incline slightly toward it. Hold the squeegee at an angle, tipping it slightly in the direction of the stroke. Retain the same angle for the entire stroke if you want the paint distributed well. Move or sway the upper part of your body in the direction of the stroke, keeping your feet wide apart for a firm, balanced base.

As the screen is raised to remove the print and to insert a new card, prop it up on the leg stand. This is a stick about 12 inches long, which dangles loosely from one side of the frame and drops down to a perpendicular position by its own weight when the frame is lifted. As this supports the frame in a steady position, the artist is free to use both hands to remove the print and set fresh stock in the register guides. When ready for printing again, release the drop stick and lower the screen. See Plate 5, Fig. *b.*

The first few prints may not be to your liking, but give yourself a chance. It will take about half a dozen prints to establish the proper relationship between the paper and the paint. Once you have the knack for it, you can easily make more than fifty impressions in an hour. Silk screen printing can be done just as rapidly as the cards can be removed from the printing base and fresh ones inserted. As each print is removed from the printing base, it is put aside to dry. Several drying facilities suitable for studio use are suggested on page 36.

Dark Moon #2 by Philip Hicken, 1956
Metropolitan Museum of Art

PLATE 34

Silk screen prints are not usually numbered to designate the total number of the edition or the state of each print. This arrangement may be desirable with printing mediums where the delicate nature of the printing plates causes the sharpness of each successive print to dim. When the plates no longer yield prints representative of the artist's best efforts, they are destroyed. The number on the print is an index of its quality in relation to the entire edition. In silk screen, which seems to violate the law of diminishing returns, the last print of an edition may be as fine in every detail as the first one, and so there is no point in listing the order of printing.

When the day's printing is over and the prints are safely stored for drying, the screen should be cleaned thoroughly. Put some old paper, the size of the printing bed, under the screen. With a sharp-edged piece of heavy cardboard about 3 inches wide and 5 inches long, scrape together any paint in the screen that has not been used. Be sure to collect the paint from all sides and corners, forming a pool of paint on one side of the screen. With another piece of cardboard held to form a V with the first, scoop up this pool of paint and put it back into the paint can. Close the can tightly. When the screen is cleared of paint, spread a soft flannel rag over the silk and pour some kerosene over it. Swish the rag around to loosen all paint in the mesh of the silk. Mop up the diluted paint with a fresh rag and repeat the kerosene treatment until there is no further evidence of paint. Wash and wipe the

Winter on the Creek by Harry Gottlieb. *Size of print 14½ by 19½ inches.*
This gay and vigorous composition was printed in nine colors. There is a continual building up of design, color upon color, and the heavy opaque white paint, printed last, gives the tangible feeling of snow.

PLATE 35

screen top and bottom. The frame, printing bed, and squeegee should also be left immaculately clean.

What would happen if paint were left on the screen? The paint would dry into a hard film. This would in time rot and crack the silk. If paint is left in the open silk, it will require a good deal of scrubbing with paint remover to get it out of the screen again. It may even be necessary to resort to a mild solution of lye and water to open the clogged mesh. No silk can long survive such treatment.

Paint that is allowed to remain on the squeegee will stiffen and rot the rubber. You will find that it is cheaper in the long run to give your tools and equipment the everyday care that they require. If you store your squeegee, see that it is not in too warm a place and be sure not to stand it up on the rubber blade. Paints should be stored in a metal closet. Kerosene-soaked rags should be held in metal cans until they can be disposed of safely.

The true artist doesn't consider cleaning up a messy job. He goes at it with a will, fully realizing its importance. Rubber gloves are not recommended because they hamper natural movement and because they in turn represent a problem in cleaning.

TROUBLE SHOOTING

In trying out this newly acquired art technique, you may meet with unforeseen problems. The following hints and suggestions should prove helpful in solving some problems that come up in the course of printing.

If your prints appear smudgy in spite of the fact that you feel you have followed all directions, check the following:

THE SCREEN

The screen may be too loose. Some stencils are affected by the weather. On humid days a glue stencil may sag and cause a wave in the screen. In printing, this wave of silk will precede the squeegee, and will cause blurred impressions. To remedy this condition, remove the paint, disengage the screen, and hold it near an electric heater for a few minutes. This should shrink the screen to its original tautness.

THE PAINT

The paint may be too thin. Paint that is soupy has a tendency to spread or crawl, and sometimes it exceeds its bounds disastrously. Running paint is particularly annoying on a print where fine lines are to be left in reverse. Unless the paint is of the right consistency, these lines will run together. To cope with this, wipe the underside of the silk with a soft flannel rag. After printing several proof sheets, notice how the trouble clears up. This is, however, only temporary relief, requiring repeated renewals of the wiping application. It is better to take the paint out of the screen, pour it back into the can, and "shorten" it by adding transparent base. Remember that as the base makes the paint thick, it will also make the color transparent. If you want to retain the original opacity, add some thick opaque paint of the same color. This will set the paint for the rest of the run.

The paint may be too heavy. When paint is too heavy, it requires strong pressure on the squeegee to push it through the silk. This increased weight may cause the silk to drag and thus result in blurred or double impressions. This problem may be solved by thinning the paint. Remove the paint from the screen and pour it back into the paint can. Add some varnish until the paint is flowing freely and does not demand excessive pressure on the squeegee. When the consistency is right, you can go ahead with the printing.

THE CONTACT

The contact necessary for good printing may become disturbed by a warped screen or by an uneven printing base. If the frame is warped in one corner, you'll have to force that part of the frame down while you squeegee, so that it lies flat against the bed. Or you might wedge up that part of the unit, by forcing cardboard underneath the bed in the warped section. In other words, the printing base may be forced up to eliminate the void between it and the frame.

If your trouble is caused by a depression in the bed, you will have to fill it in with strips of gummed paper. First glue on a strip of gummed paper as large as the hollow and then add smaller and smaller strips in a steplike arrangement. When the hollow has been filled, cover the entire printing bed with a smooth heavy sheet of cardboard and fasten the guides on top of this in their usual position.

It is important that the printing bed be not only level and flat, but also smooth. The thin paper used for most fine-art prints is sensitively receptive to any roughness on the bed. Any unevenness will interfere with the smooth application of color. The bed should be sanded down to allow for easy sliding of the paper into the guides as well as for smooth printing. After the bed is sanded down, some talcum powder dusted over the surface will help to speed up the registration of cards in the guides.

PINHOLES

If there are any pinholes in the stencil, minute dots of paint will show up on the prints. These are most likely to develop in glue and photographic screens after long use. It is an easy matter to stop out these pinholes. Remove the paint from the screen and wash the screen with turpentine, which dries pretty fast. When you hold the clean screen against the light, you can see all the spots that have to be touched up. Use black lacquer, glue, shellac, or tempera color for this purpose. Black lacquer is best because it is most visible and dries the fastest.

If, judging from a spotty print, you see that there are just a handful of pinholes, you do not have to go through the entire procedure of removing the paint and cleaning the screen. Merely stand the screen up on its prop and stop out the pinholes on the underside of the silk. When the touched-up parts are dry, continue the printing.

RIPPED SILK

Ordinarily the same silk screen will last for thousands of prints. But everything seems to happen to the beginner, and chances are that a rip in the silk will be his first major calamity. A tear in the silk may be caused by a tack or some other sharp object having fallen into the paint or screen. It may be caused by an unseen pin in a wiping cloth or even by a nail scratch during cleaning. If the rip is small and does not appear close to or within the printing area, it is a minor calamity and can be patched up. Remove all paint from the screen and wash the silk carefully with turpentine. Take two pieces of newspaper slightly larger than the rip and lacquer them. While the lacquer is wet, use these strips to patch the silk on both sides. Be certain that the patches and the silk between them are all in close contact. When the lacquer adhesive patch is dry, the screen is again ready for use. The silk will be as good as new but can be used only as long as the injured area is not a part of the open area of a stencil design.

If the rip comes within the printing area, the printing has to be stopped, new silk stretched across the frame, and the stencil remade.

OTHER HELPFUL HINTS

Sometimes when printing on paper you find that, as the screen is lifted after squeegeeing, the print clings to the silk. When the paper is pulled away from the screen, it is dragged a little and may cause smudges in the print. You may find one of these two suggestions helpful in such a situation. One is to make the paint thinner and less sticky. The other is to attach clips to the register guides to hold the paper on the base as the screen is raised. The stock is fed into the guides as usual. Clips may be thin cardboard, strong manila paper, or celluloid, extending about 1/4 inch onto the paper.

If you have trouble steadying the squeegee against the frame when you're not using it, here is a handy trick to know. Nail two narrow strips of cardboard or wood 1 by 5 inches across the squeegee casing so that they extend wing-like over the front and back of the squeegee. These *butterflies* will support the squeegee wherever it may be and keep it from getting smudged with paint. See Plate 2.

If your squeegee is almost as wide as the frame, here is another hint for keeping it from falling into the paint. Hammer two 3-inch nails or pegs into the squeegee casing so that the nails protrude from both ends of the casing like roasting spits. These pegs should be inserted at such a level on the casing that when you are not holding the squeegee, they will rest on the frame, supporting the squeegee.

TABLE OF SOLVENTS

MEDIUM	SOLVENT
Glue	Water
Lacquer	Lacquer thinner (acetate)
Shellac	Alcohol
Tusche	
When dry	Kerosene, turpentine
When wet	Water
Oil color	Kerosene, turpentine
Tempera color	Water
Enamel	Kerosene, turpentine
Lacquer film	Lacquer thinner (acetate)
Photo transfer film	Lye-water mixture

SOURCES OF SUPPLY

Your local art dealer is your best source of supply and a good source of information. We recommend that you visit him and discuss your supply problem with him. He may be found in the classified directory under the following categories: Silk Screen Supplies, Screen Supplies, Artist's Materials, Process Supplies.

In the absence of any local source, the following list of specialized dealers will be helpful; many will supply a catalog upon request.

Active Process Supply Co., 15 W. 20 St., New York, N. Y. 10011

Advance Process Supply Co., 400 N. Noble St., Chicago, Ill. 60622

Atlas Silk Screen Supply Co., 1733 N. Milwaukee Ave., Chicago, Ill. 60647

Cincinnati Screen Process Supplies, Inc., 1111 Meta Dr., Cincinnati, Ohio 45237

Colonial Process Supply Co., 180 E. Union Ave., Rutherford, N. J. 07073

Craftint Manufacturing Co., 18501 Euclid Ave., Cleveland, Ohio 44112

Bert L. Daily, Inc., 120 E. 3 St., Dayton, Ohio 45402

Ernst W. Dorn Co., Inc., 15905 Broadway, Gardena, Calif. 90247

McLogan's Sign Painters Supply House, 1324 S. Hope St., Los Angeles, Calif. 90015

Naz-Dar Co., 1087 N. Branch, Chicago, Ill. 60622

Nu-Film Products Co., 56 W. 22 St., New York, N. Y. 10010

Joseph E. Podgor Co., Inc., Airport Circle and Industrial Park, Pennsauken, N. J. 08110

Serascreen Corp., 5-25 47 Rd., Long Island City, N. Y. 11101

Silk Screen Supplies, Inc., 33 Lafayette Ave., Brooklyn, N. Y. 11217

Southwestern Process Supply Co., 120 E. Main, Tulsa, Okla. 74103

Ulano Companies, 210 E. 86 St., New York, N. Y. 10028

Union Ink Co., Inc., 453 Broad Ave., Ridgefield, N. J. 07657

For current news, books, and advertisements concerning the silk-screen process and techniques, consult the *Screen Process Magazine,* the trade periodical of the industry, published by the Signs of the Times Publishing Co., 407 Gilbert Ave., Cincinnati, Ohio.

INDEX